UnBreakable

I

The First 10 Reasons Why People Go Broke Despite Working

Brad Kong

"UnBrokable*** may be not a word we can find in a dictionary yet, as I coined it: **A person who cannot be broke, financially.**"

— Prologue in *UnBrokable*

Disclaimer

These are the full title and subtitle of this book:

UnBrokable* I:
The 1st 10 Reasons Why People Go **Broke** Despite Working

I wrote only "**The 1st 10 Reasons Why Broke**" on the front cover *intentionally* for rhyme, simplicity and focus.

The graphic on this book cover is from Edit.org. I use the site to design my covers; it provides book cover templates with its copy-righted images to writers who paid "annual memberships." I do have three proofs of my membership to Edit.org, payment receipt for the membership through Paypal and reference address to the image of the site. I am writing this because I received emails regarding my "book cover images" twice; both of which were resolved within a day. I decided to stick to my own or edit.org's images since I cannot keep getting copyright emails. If you have any issue regarding my cover art, feel free to contact me: I will be more than happy to provide the three proofs again.

Copyright © 2025 Brad Kong

All rights reserved. No part of this book may be reproduced or used in any manner without the prior written permission of the copyright owner, except for the use of brief quotations in a book review.

Also by Brad Kong

UnBrokable* series:

UnBrokable I* (Chapter 1 to 10)

Preliminary series:

*Introduction to UnBrokable**
UnBrokable I* (Chapter 1 to 10)
UnBrokable II* (Chapter 11 to 20)
UnBrokable III* (Chapter 21 to 30)
UnBrokable IV* (Chapter 31 to 40)
UnBrokable* V (Chapter 41 to 50)
UnBrokable* VI (Chapter 51 to 60)
UnBrokable* VII (Chapter 61 to 70)
UnBrokable* VIII (Chapter 71 to 80)
*UnBrokable** (Chapter 1 to 80)

Drafts series:

*Introduction to UnBrokable** (Chapter 1 to 5)
Intro to UnBrokable Large Print*
UnBrokable I* (Chapter 1 to 10)
UnBrokable II* (Chapter 11 to 20)
UnBrokable III* (Chapter 21 to 30)
UnBrokable IV* (Chapter 31 to 40)
UnBrokable V* (Chapter 41 to 50)
UnBrokable VI* (Chapter 51 to 60)
UnBrokable VII* (Chapter 61 to 70)
UnBrokable VIII* (Chapter 71 to 80)
*UnBrokable** (Chapter 1 to 80)

Brad Short Story Collection I:

Robbery at Cyb Knight

How to Get Rid of Ladies
11 Girls I had Loved
Say No To TSLA
3 Ways to Avoid Divorce
15 Ways to Keep Your Teeth Healthy
5 Moments When I Felt Sorry For My Cat
Corn Dog Grandpas
Condo Chronicle
How to Lose 40 Pounds

Brad Short Story Collection II:

15 Things You Didn't Know About Korea
3 Reasons Why We Need to Buy a Home Early
Why Are CDs Super Important?
Say No To TSLA (2nd Edition)
Large Pizza for $5
30 Reasons Why I am Great
3 Reasons Why the Nursing Home Filed Bankruptcy
3 Mistakes Offline Small Business Owners Make
3 Lessons I have Learned from the Stock Market
My Friend Soo-young

Brad Short Story Collection III:

Brad Short Story Collection I & II
Why Are Orcas Friendly to Humans?
30 Reasons Why I am Lucky
30 Little Things Making Me Happy

Quotist:

Quotist I
Quotist II
Quotist III
Quotist IV
Quotist V
Quotist

Praise for *UnBrokable*

"This is the best book I have ever read. I am saying this only because Brad is my husband."

-Tsina D,
A housewife and teacher

"I cannot believe my dad wrote this much thick book. He must be a genius."

-Yuna K,
An elementary school student

"I am proud of my son who wrote a book in English."

-Ms. Jin,
A wealthy woman

"Publishing this book is a celebration itself. Write your name on the next page if you bought this for a gift."

-Brad K,
A philosopher, writer, publisher, book designer and investor

UnBrokable*

Dear _____

This book is my gift for you.
It has been helpful for me, so I hope it will be helpful for you as well.
Thank you always.
Sincerely,

From _____BRAD_____

I would appreciate if you leave an Amazon review!

For all the hard *Workers*
Struggling Everyday

Contents

Prologue

1. Drinking and Smoking

2. Having Too Many Children

3. Getting into Debt Too Easily

4. Not Using Systems Already Paid for

5. Triple Spending Lifestyle

6. Living in an Expensive Area

7. Social Media Addiction

8. Having a Bad Reputation

9. Making Yourself Undesirable

10. Marrying a Spouse without Income

Author's Note

Prologue

*Dying poor is a shame, especially in wealthy countries.
It is not about money – it shows how we have lived.*
-Brad Kong

This is me sitting on a Ferrari in Miami, FL (2003) – wasting parents' money thoughtlessly. I didn't expect to go broke abysmally, then.

What does make a person poor? Why do some people still rent an APT, even after 30 years of employment? Maybe some are destitute because of social injustice or political corruption; nonetheless, shouldn't we do anything about it? My name is Brad and I have been a small business owner, nursing home dishwasher and stock investor in the last 25 years.

"DJ Ye-song" is a 23-year-old K-pop star – who got sentenced to *8 years to jail* in Dec, 2024 – after *her* drunk driving caused a manslaughter. It's *hapless* for a girl to spend her prime in prison due to drinking. The other day, I watched a documentary about "lonely death," increasing in Korea. A lot of adults are living alone in *micro apts* there – unmarried, divorced or widowed – and die alone, occasionally. It focused on a deceased lady in her 40s and I checked again that there is *alcoholism* behind most suicides; she didn't have enough savings, but simultaneously kept drinking *soju* and passed away. After all, it's not exactly that the poor end their lives – more likely, the *alcoholic* do it after getting impoverished.

Jack Whittaker was a construction firm owner in Putnam County, WV – known as the winner of a lottery jackpot of $315 M in 2002. He was a millionaire already with a net worth of $17 M before the win – in a word, a rich man won a bonanza. Oddly, a series of unfortunate events happened to him afterwards. First, a guy named Tribble, the boyfriend of Whittaker's granddaughter Brandi, was found dead of OD in Whittaker's home in 2004; three months later, Brandi herself was also found dead at 17 – cocaine and methadone were found in her body. Five years later, Bragg, who was Whittaker's daughter and the mother of Brandi, was also found deceased at 42 in Daniels, WV. Then, Whittaker's home in Bland County was reported to be on fire in 2016. Finally, Mr. Whittaker himself passed away following an illness at 72 in 2020: Why did the luckiest guy in the world have to go through all those miseries?

Hamas from Palestine attacked Israel in Oct 2023 – a war broke out instantly. If I were Israelis, I wouldn't try to expand my territory against Palestinians. In reality, **most land in Israel doesn't have commercial values – no oil, agriculture or water resources.** I may keep some lands near Tel Aviv (still several times bigger than Hong Kong or Singapore) and try to build a city like Dubai there; I wouldn't fight over useless lands against Palestinians. The fact that we don't think practically can be another reason for poverty. *Land* used to have "absolute values" in farming, a rather *ancient concept*, not applicable any more. The *point* is to obtain safe territory for the Jewish to settle and virtually 80% of Australia or Canada are empty. I wonder what Moses would do if he governs now – by the time he led the Exodus out of Egypt, new continents were not discovered yet.

Han Liu was a Chinese billionaire, the former chairman of Hanlong group in mining. His net worth was claimed at $6 B by the time he passed away at 49 in 2015. He was convicted of murdering 8 people, while running a mafia style gang for his business, making him executed by the law enforcement in China. His last words were viral: "Life is short; *we don't have to live too diligently for more money*. I will have a small store and live happily with my family next life." In *Psychology of money*, there was a man named Read, who had been a janitor for 42 years, made a fortune out of blue-chip stocks, left $8 M to a hospital and passed away. I know a similar case of Groner, who had been a secretary for 43 years, made profit out of the ABT stock, left $7 M to a college and died. They were undoubtedly honorable, but frankly, *what's the point?* As long as I have enough, I concluded **the best reward I can give to myself is *working less*.**

Have you ever been a dishwasher before? If you don't completely agree with this book, it's possible that you might not have been *broke* enough. I believe the ultimate way to avoid indigence is to stay away from the reasons causing it. While working in a nursing home, I observed that some seniors complain their children never visit. It's not entirely the children's fault. For 7 years, I saw some elderly residents, who were aggressive on staff, never got a visitor. I also remember we had a woman cook, especially rude to dishwashers, who got divorced three times after having five kids. *The same goes for money:* "*Not* being *helpful*" can make anyone insolvent in the end.

* * *

UnBrokable* is not a word in a dictionary yet, as I coined it, meaning **a person who cannot be broke financially**. This series might not be for the super-rich, but for **unlucky people who have no idea how to get out of poverty** – an unorthodox guide to stay away from **brokeness**[1] (not having enough). Have

---

[1] Don't get confused with "*brokenness,*" meaning "a condition in which something is badly damaged."

you been *broke* before, despite working full time? If someone is deprived despite working to death, there could be reasons. It is a simple misconception that "Working hard makes us rich." In fact, it *can make us poorer,* as some exhaust themselves that way. I am a middle-aged man with my wife and daughter and my American life has been divided into four periods since 1999.

1. Schools: Cornell and SUNY at Buffalo (1999-2005)
2. Business: Cyb Knight Video Games (2006-2014)
3. Employment: A nursing home (2015-2022)
4. Investor and writer (2022 - current)

Or I can divide my last 25 years by careers:

- College banquet (1999 - 2002)
- eBay seller (2003 - 2015)
- Cyb Knight manager (2006-2014)
- Nursing home dishwasher (2015-2022)
- Investor and writer (2011-current)

I earned two American certificates, while working in the nursing home: medical coder and pharmacy technician. And I have worked for diverse *small jobs* since high school, including convenience store clerk, bar kitchen helper, military soldier, etc.

* * *

Out of all those jobs, the latest *dishwasher* gave me the inspiration to write *UnBrokable* series.* The nursing home I worked at is within walking distance from my home. I had a chance to volunteer one day in 2015, which brought me a permanent *weekend position, unexpectedly* (then, I hadn't done anything for a year after closing out my store in 2014). At the end of the work, the chef suddenly "wondered," if I could do the job at least during the weekends. Now I see the reason why, as nursing homes are always short of staff. Since they suggested a good hourly rate and plenty of free food from the kitchens, I accepted that offer. I had the job *only on weekends* for seven years.

I have never liked the job since it was physically hard, but admit that it was helpful somehow. Above all, I had chances to meet people I wouldn't have without it. I believe I was able to see reasons why some workers got stuck – **causes to keep them in chains.** Secondly, the job brought me more physical strength and weight loss. Thirdly, those extra wages, bonus and free food allowed me to build up my savings faster. There could be obvious reasons why some go broke (e.g., gambling). On the contrary, **there are people** apparently not doing anything wrong, but **consistently being broke, while working full.**

While I owned the video game store, my daughter was born in 2010. When a baby is born, parents need more cash, while physically exhausted. Incidentally, *the mortgage bubble* burst in 2007 and severe depression came in 2009. While I had wasted tons of my parents' money only to keep my store open, the only good thing I did was *buying* a condo *in full.* Since the economy crashed, there were plenty of foreclosures, short sales and discounted houses on the market – getting rid of rent and mortgage for good was the only advantage I took during the era.

After being impecunious myself and watching others struggle, I started wondering what makes laborers in trouble – any **trap punishing full-timers,** despite wealth in the nation? The dishwashers who rented APTs for 30 years, frequently worked *double*, staying up to 15 hours a day: *Where did all their money go?* All the episodes in this book are from my own experiences or true events throughout history. By the time we reach the epilogue, I hope we will be more mature, knowledgeable and close to wealthy.

1

Drinking and Smoking

*All the poverties in the world originate
from drinking and smoking.*
- Brad Kong

Alexander the Great (356 – 323 BC) was an emperor of the Greek kingdom of Macedonia, who had created the largest empires in European history; his territory stretched from Egypt to northern India, then. He was known to be *undefeated* in battles and considered the greatest military commander. While he had lived a successful life in general, his sudden downfall seemed to come with his heavy drinking. The ruler impulsively killed "Cleitus the Black," who saved Alexander's life once at a battle, during a violent drunken altercation; it shows that Cleitus accused him of judgmental mistakes that night. The monarch deeply regretted the accident, but his severe alcoholism likely started from that point. Alexander swam one day and developed a mild fever possibly due to malaria; he spent more days only on binge drinking and passed away – he was 32-years-old.

    Yoon is the 13th president of South Korea elected in 2022. He was a prosecutor general previously, but he has an interesting record of failing bar exams 9 times straight; in other words, it took 10 years for him to pass the legal test after college. Passing a bar exam is not easy, yet I believe most law students in college pass it after failing a couple times in Korea (Kim Kardashian passed it after failing three times, while taking care of four kids). Coincidentally, this president is known for his *chronic alcoholism*; he was in office barely over 2 years (out of 5), got impeached in April, 2025 and is in jail now (as of August, 2025). Some believe his numerous failures and early termination were due to his heavy drinking habit, likely started when he was in college.

James Cook was a British explorer and the captain of the Royal Navy in the 18th century. He has been known for his voyages to New Zealand and Australia across the Pacific Ocean – finding sea routes never known before and discovering unknown islands. He also visited Hawaii as the first westerner in 1778. When the navy returned to Hawaii the next year, it shows the military had a surprising welcome reception from the natives. Incidentally, it was a Hawaiian festival period to worship Polynesian god Lono and they mistakenly believed James was the deity who returned; the British decided to stay on the island for a month. Soon after, though, it turned out that the captain and crews had been drunk all the time, had fist fights with natives and harassed island women – the anger of the Hawaiians had grown. One day, both parties had an exceptionally big quarrel over stuff stolen by Hawaiians from the English boats; the captain Cook tried to capture the King of Hawaii, "Kalaniʻōpuʻu" as a hostage, but failed. Regretfully, he was stabbed to death at 50 in 1779.

Did you know that it takes a lot of harvests to make a little amount of alcohol? That is why the Korean Joseon dynasty had occasional *prohibition eras*, whenever famines came. In a sense, making alcohol can be a global waste; drinking can promote our society to waste grains and fruits. I believe money drain starts from drinking, smoking or frequently both – the *most prevalent and common*. **It is important to stop draining, before trying to figure out how to make more.**

* * *

Amy Winehouse was an English singer and songwriter. She was 27 when she died of her noted alcoholism in London, England in 2011 – her net worth was about $4 M. Verne Troyer was an American comedian – best known for his role of "Mini-Me" in the *Austin Powers*. He died at 49 in Los Angeles, CA in 2018 (an alcohol poisoning); he was just about to get noticed after a long obscurity in his career. I have always thought that drinking and smoking are the biggest wastes, including *time*: 'I have wasted decades of my life, but I have never done it on drinking, at least.'

The *weekend* dishwashing job I had was like a Siberian death camp over the winter. I finished my army service by 1997, and still I don't see anything else I can compare it with. Countless people quit it within a week and a few even quit within 30 minutes. I truly wondered how some were able to keep it full-time for decades in that huge nursing home. There were *a couple of old Mexicans* who were unpleasant yet diligent. Quite frankly, the amount of wages, tips and bonuses I had received was far more than I expected. Besides, they gave me plenty of free food from the five restaurants inside, continuously (I didn't have to go to supermarkets for months at a point). Since most people spend their salaries on food, the job was actually a deal. I assumed it was how those Latinos were able to support their five children by dishwashing – along with other benefits as full-time workers, too. **Regardless, the two were still renting apartments at the age of 60: *Why?*** There is an excerpt from the *Talmud*: A Jewish student asked, "Why are our pupils dark?" A rabbi answered that, "It is better for us to see the dark side of life first."

* * *

Sadly, three ladies committed suicide together in Seoul, Korea in 2014: one mother and two daughters – not common, considering all the victims were grown-ups. Apparently, they burned coal in their small room, causing carbon monoxide poisoning. The mother was a 60-years old *eatery worker* and got laid off a month before this pact. The two daughters were in their 30s; the elder was unemployed due to diabetes; the younger had a part time job at a graphic novel publisher, but suffered from small wage, debt and bad credit. This tragedy shocked the nation for a month, then. No one understood why this family could not get any support from the government. Eventually, the police concluded that the reason was financial hardship. Investigators and reporters checked the house thoroughly and found a grocery check book by the mother in the end. Not everyone writes all the spending thoroughly like her, so I could see that she had been conscientious.

Nonetheless, I couldn't help that a few items in their lists grabbed my attention: soju ($4.40), cigarettes ($20) and beers ($1.90 and $1.95). I thought that they passed away solely due to lack of money. I had been desperate myself, but in my case, I couldn't waste a single cent for a few years. Soju is a cheap but popular drink in Korea – merely a diluted ethanol with sweetener (a small bottle is about $10 from Amazon). Different from wine or beer, it does not have any taste at all except chemical –

actually, Americans complained it tastes just like ethanol from a chemistry lab. I believe it was invented when the country was a ruin after the Korean war in the 1950s, as it did not have much harvest to make a drink properly. Unexplainably, it is still a favorite among the poor.

Nevertheless, I suddenly felt different as soon as I saw these in their purchases – feeling like they called for obvious consequences. **Were drinking and smoking the reason making them broke from the start?** After all, soju is not a food we need to survive: in fact, it's not even a drink – merely a chemical. They could have saved "that $28.25" in their pocket in 2014; little things change our lives in destitution. More importantly, alcohol is known to cause depression, leading to suicides.

* * *

 The last dynasty in the Korean peninsula was the Joseon (1392–1897). It had had several *Prohibition eras* officially recorded and **the penalty for the violation was death** – cutting heads by a machete. The record says that an official named Yun was decapitated in the 16th century: "People are starved to death, as there is no grain during famine. No one can eat a bag of rice, all at once. **Yet people can drink up a jar of alcohol overnight, made out of a bag of rice**" (too much rice to make a small amount of alcohol).

A popular Korean YouTube lady pointed out that all the expensive alcohols come out of the body as *urine* after all. I also watched a documentary about a fallen celebrity in Korea – a man who used to be a top singer 20 years ago, but is poor now. It shows that he still wears a $10,000 coat and drinks $200 beers. One lady commented that, "The expensive clothes will stay, but beers will go away." Alcohol is beyond *useless,* damaging organs, but the truth is that virtually all types of drinks[2] except water is bad for our teeth – as a result, water is the only liquid I put in my mouth personally.

I watched a documentary about Angel Falls in Venezuela the other day – heavy rainfall drops on top of the mountain daily, which is why the tops are flat by beats. Then, water comes down through the falls, goes to streams, rivers and all the way to the oceans. **Drinking and smoking are similar to those rainfalls;** these two may create minor problems in the beginning, but can continue all the way to oceans of bigger ones (e.g. liver failure). Another analogy can be the human population. If all the problems are the eight billion human population, drinking and smoking could be a couple of *Australopithecus* 4 million years ago. Some think they are still wealthy despite those, but for sure, they could have been better without them. When I was in college in Korea, I lived in a home-stay in 1992. The brother of the landlady complained he forgot $2,000 cash somewhere, while he was drinking the other night.

The issues of drinking and smoking start with draining cash – continuing on DUI fines, fighting, losing teeth, concussion or kidney malfunctions, etc. There is a Chinese foot massage place near my home, owned by a middle aged couple. I used to feel sorry for them since massaging feet must be boring, even with small charges. I saw them closing their door one night – they went straight to the liquor store across the street. 'Well, do they have money for that?' I pondered. **While I owned my video game store, I didn't have a cent to waste,** as I had lost little every month all the way throughout the eight years of the ownership. The couple never understood drinking could be the reason why they got stuck. I have never tried the place since it looked deteriorating; window decals were wearing off; I felt the business sinking with their habits. When owners don't drink and

---

[2] Soda, juice, coffee, etc.

smoke, their store looks fresher even from outside, as I know what my shop looked like.

* * *

I was a freshman in high school in Korea in 1989. Then, the college entrance exam was exceedingly competitive and getting private tutoring from college students was common. Korea was poorer and tutorings were not expensive; a lot of college students did it for part time jobs. One day, my mother brought a college student for my tutoring. When I think about it now, she was not wise; as a result, I ended up getting only lessons the whole day, instead of studying on my own; she is not the type of person who decides things on her own, but always did what others do, blindly (which I hate). Anyway, the guy attended mechanical engineering in Seoul National, the most prestigious in Korea (like Harvard in America). Unfortunately, his lessons were awful and not helpful for my grades at all. Above all, he had a violent unpleasant character, not a teacher material, to begin with.

However, my parents were greedy and thought it was the best for my brother and me. I felt like they considered us as the future incomes; brother and I should get better grades and jobs, so we can support them stably later on? Anyway, that guy was from Busan, far from Seoul. Eventually, except me, all of our family *agreed* that he should stay in our house for his own college and our tutoring. When I think about it now, that guy was nothing more than a garbage. Even though he was only 22, he smoked crazily. One day, my smoker father visited his room and was shocked by how much cigarette odor was stuck in his room. Since our home was far from his college even in Seoul, I recall that he skipped his classes a lot; later, the guy complained that he got five F's during a semester since he made a lot of effort to teach us (nonsense). Simply, he was a terrible student himself not doing his job - **he failed because of him.**

What shocked me later was that his parents turned out to be extremely wealthy. My mother's hometown is also Busan, so I had a chance to visit his home, while I visited my grandma. I was surprised at the size of the house. I still remember he once complained that his parents got $8 M fine from the IRS after an audit; which was believable considering the house. But, as a result of his poor grades, I heard he could not study abroad in America, despite his parents' fortune. Korea is wealthier now, but still is a small, but monotonous country. A lot of people are eager to get out of there for numerous reasons. In his case, his seriously bad grades were the reason to block him from getting opportunities. When I found him online in 2016, he seemed to own an English kindergarten in Korea *(a shame)*. I guess the only job experience he had was tutoring, so he might have gone for it. I found out that his mother was a pharmacist when I was at his house (seemingly, both of his parents studied well); I never liked that guy since he was physically violent to us – after all, a loser who wasted youth on heavy smoking.

The reason why drinking and smoking are horrible is for their long term effects (health issues); as a result, we can end up spending way more during life time. Even for the super rich, our bodies are the most important assets. An asset is something that brings money to us, and wealth building starts with protecting the most fundamental ones. As Emerson said, "the first *wealth* is *health*."

***

Summary

1. If you are serious about getting out of poverty, quit drinking and smoking first.
2. These two can connect us to millions of other headaches.
3. These two consume time, too.

2

Having too Many Children

The human population does not have to be bigger than it is now.
-Brad Kong

Charles Dickens (1812-1870) was an English author who wrote *Oliver Twist* and *A Christmas Carol*. He and his wife Catherine married in 1836, when Charles was 24 and she was 21. From then until the time of their divorce 22 years later, *Catherine gave birth to 10 children*. It shows that Dickens' own childhood had been bitter. At the age of 12, with his father imprisoned for debt, he had to work in a shoe factory, pasting labels on jars of shoe polish for a few shillings each week – by then, his parents had eight children and Charles was the second.

Although I don't personally expect my daughter would be a good money maker, which is perfectly fine, it seems Dickens had thought differently. Unhappily, none of his children turned out to be a successful writer like him and he publicly lamented that, "having brought up the largest family ever known with the smallest talents to do anything." In other words, he had to virtually pay everything for family until he passed away. Dickens grew miserable about his breeding eventually: The history recorded that **he resented the fact that he had so many children to support**. And, ironically, somehow, he saw it as his wife's fault. He didn't approve of Catherine's lack of energy, and began to indicate that she had never been his intellectual equal. In June 1858, Charles and Catherine filed for divorce (rare then) and he started seeing a new woman named Turnan.

I have only one child, partly because I had a hard time, financially: Isn't it logical, though? No money, so I decided not to have more than I could afford. Unfortunately, to me, a lot of people (especially poor ones) don't seem to think the same. Some give births no matter what and fortify their poverty – almost looking like **they make sure to be broke for the rest of their lives.**

* * *

Dreadfully, Jennifer and Sarah Hart murdered their *six* children by driving the family's SUV off a cliff in Mendocino County, CA in 2018; all eight people were in the vehicle during the accident. Police found the bodies of seven in or near the crashed vehicle; the county judge ruled that the body of one missing child was in the vehicle at the time of the crash, so a death certificate was signed on him as well. Toxicology results showed that Jennifer's blood alcohol content was over the limit; Sarah and two children had Benadryl in their bodies. Sarah had made Google searches about "the lethality of Benadryl" and "the nature of death by drowning"; her searches also included "No-kill shelters for dogs," as the family had two. Apparently, this suicide had been planned in advance; it showed Sarah telling her co-worker that she wished someone told, "It is okay not to have a big family by adoption"; Wiki shows the couple had been struggling with and physically abusing their children for years.

It was *noble* for the couple to adopt orphans, initially – one way to take care of kids who need help without increasing our population. Still, they should have granted that taking care of children is extremely hard: *No reason to go too ambitious about it.* This adoption case is different from producing too many babies, as there are people having so many children no matter what (including Latin Americans). After the success of *"Jon and Kate plus 8"* shows, there are more couples giving birth to sextuplets and putting them on TV.

Personally, **I don't consider producing a lot of babies as an *accomplishment***; especially, there is nothing much for men to do to make that happen; at least, women have to go through pregnancy and labor, but what does a man do exactly? Eating a lot of food is not an achievement; sleeping long is not an attainment. From a point of view, all of these are just results caused by irresponsibilities due to not controlling basic instincts.

* * *

I watched a documentary about poor senior citizens in Korea the other day; suicide rate in the country is the highest among OECD[3]s in the past two decades (especially among the elderly after retirements). They interviewed a grandpa who had been a construction painter for life. He lived in a small room in a decaying residence and said he watches TV all day and eats a small rice porridge twice a day from a convenience store; he and his wife had raised three children there, though they all moved out as adults. Suddenly, this idea hit me: *"If he had only one child instead of three, could things have been different?"* It costs a lot to raise one there. Subsequently, I've wondered, "Korea is super crowded now – more every year. Was it necessary for him to have even one?" The human population is increasing fast everywhere on Earth now: **More than ever**. This may be something we need to consider before moving on to the next level.

To me, having too many children *blindly* can be even a sin; at least, it can be selfish, as **our survival heavily depends on the death of other animals.** As much as our lives are important, their lives matter, too. I strictly do not eat chicken, but over 50 billion chickens are slaughtered every year; others are butchered as well, including cows, pigs, sheep, goats, ducks, fishes, etc; certainly, livestock are not the only ones killed by humans. Human population is expected to be over 9.2 billion by 2040, according to the Director of National Intelligence –

---

[3] Organization for Economic Co-operation and Development – 38 wealthiest countries in the world.

meaning **over 1 billion more humans will be created and added on top of the current in the next 17 years** – an extremely fast increase in any standard. People often suffer when they give birth and raise children physically or financially; I don't see a visible need for us to go through more pains while struggling.

I saw an Indonesian lady's video on YouTube the other day. She was the wife of a Korean man and the couple had made tons of foods on a regular basis and donated them to poor children in Bali, supposed to be humanitarian. One day, the couple bought a fat pig (150 lb.) to kill and cook. The lady was so elated with a big smile and tried to carry the pig with giggling and laughter with villagers, while the pig was screaming to death (*horrific scream*). I felt disgusted by her mindset: "Only humans matter and nothing else." We ought to change our attitudes, as **humans won't last long by being offensive:** Changing our views is the ultimate way we can make our existence a little longer. There is a movie titled *Brokeback Mountain* starring Gyllenhaal and Ledger; in a restaurant scene, poor L cried, "You forgot what it's like being *broke* all the time." The rich G had one child and the poor L had three (2 girls and 1 stepchild). There is an old legend called *Heung-bu* in Korea, starring two brothers; the old was rich and the younger was poor. The rich was childless, but the poor had nine. *Do we need to have a lot in this era?*

The human population was about 300 million in the year of 1 (AD 1[4]), according to *8 Billion and Counting* by Scuibba. Now it is about 8 billion in 2023, representing 7% of the total humans ever born on Earth – about 108 billion people have been born and died throughout evolution. Along with DNI, the U.N. also projected that the human population will be over 9 billion by 2040 – *an exponential growth.* For sure, this explosion has never happened on this planet before. Delivering and raising a child is hard work for everyone, requiring a lot of sacrifices, too.

---

[4] When Jesus Christ was born.

When we sacrifice ourselves, someone (else) should get benefit out of it, at least: Do you agree? Otherwise, all of our sacrifices go in vain. However, have you ever thought that **no one gets benefit out of our rapid population growth?** What if we sacrifice for nothing? Is it possible that the Earth gets hurt or resources are depleted faster not "in spite of", but "because of" our stupid *"sacrifice?"*

* * *

Have you ever considered that having too many kids can be a reason for a divorce? It's highly likable, according to my experience; it is important since a majority of people file bankruptcies, thanks to divorces. I *used to* wonder why some parents get divorced, long after having three kids; it takes several years to have 3; they would have known each other well enough, before reaching that many. Now, as a parent, I reasonably suspect that *having too many kids itself may be the reason for a divorce*: For example, it is statistically true that **mothers with twins have higher rates of divorces in America**; which get higher when parents have bigger multiplets. The same marriage can be vastly different, depending on the kid numbers.

In a sense, getting married is similar to getting a job, especially for full-time housewives. It can be heaven to hell, depending on the number of kids, as, for me, taking care of one has been an enormous amount of work. Certainly, marriage life can be hell to heaven *based on a lot of things*: The difference is that we can still control how many kids we have, at least. We can inherit hardships from our parents, often uncontrollable. Still, in my case, I was able to decide how many I have: **We don't have to create hardships for ourselves,** when we have a choice.

Do you know how to avoid a divorce? From *my point of view as a husband*, home should be a *livable place* for a wife. In other words, a pleasant marriage means the amount of work in a household should be doable; at least, it shouldn't be a hellish amount for a wife. Otherwise, it is more probable that she feels like giving it up, which happened to me in my previous jobs. Certainly, a wife can still endure large amounts of work without complaining, but *why is that necessary?* What if we have a choice to make situations easier? Isn't it better for a wife to get little amounts of work? Isn't it *even better* if she does little while her husband is rich? Statistically, fewer women file divorces in better conditions, as **the job of a housewife is not strikingly different from ones outside.** It is husbands' judgment to set up livable conditions and avoid divorces. Imagine your home is a restaurant (home is also a place to make and serve foods). Which restaurant would you like to work at? A or B?

A

B

(Image source: random free photos online)

If the two households have the same incomes, I would choose "A." Some cafes have a crazy amount of customers with a lot of things to do; still, when owners pay employees well with benefits, many laborers stay; these are usually upscale restaurants. In another type, pay is barely minimum, but they have a small amount of work to do. I have seen employees stay for decades in this type of restaurant in big hospitals or nursing homes (huge medical facilities may have several joints inside). I used to work in one of those only for breakfast – the *easiest job* I ever had, because not many eat breakfasts, to begin with. Unless caring for more salary, working there only four hours in the morning was ideal for me; the dining management didn't care much about sales or the number of guests eating; the facility made money out of caregiving, instead. I think my current home is similar to this situation: I cannot bring a huge income, yet my wife has less things to do with a child.

On the other hand, most restaurants on the streets don't (can't) pay employees a lot, while having too many things to do. So many servers quit on a weekly basis there; employee turnover is high and labor shortages are constant. I believe most families (60%), having wives with jobs and two children, are in this condition; the high employee quitting rates in those are similar to the high divorce rates in America. Conclusively, the most ideal option for a wife is that she gets paid a lot, while having a tiny amount of work. Still, a poor husband (like me) can try to make the condition that his wife has little things to do: *Planning wisely from the start could be cheaper than going through divorces.* Then, how can I decrease the amount of work? One way is having fewer babies – one in my case. **What blocks you from having *fewer* babies?** Personally, I do not see a disadvantage when my wife has less chores; frankly, whenever outside, I feel less guilty when I know she's busy with one at home, rather than more.

* * *

I honestly do not know how others can take care of more than *one*. I used to take my daughter everywhere by the time she got into elementary: libraries, zoos, museums, aquariums, restaurants, etc. I spent plenty of time with her outside during the summers and felt good about myself – *what a great dad I am!* "I am such a great husband to give my wife enough time to take a rest." Unfortunately, it did *not last* long; I got exhausted after doing that for a few years. Now it has been several years that only my wife has taken care of my daughter exclusively; I just do not have energy any more to play with my daughter, not to mention bring her out, which actually requires a lot of energy. Fortunately, we have a nice young lady next door and my daughter spends time with her frequently; more luckily, her mother visits every summer and brings my daughter out to the farmer's market, etc. So four adults take care of a child now and seemingly it really takes a village to raise a child. I am not sure if I am particularly bad with child rearing – all I know is I am very tired.

I think raising a child is hard in two aspects – physical and financial. I am from a wealthy family and got multiple financial support from my parents, but the cost has not been as cheap as I expected in the beginning. One question to myself, considering the second child: *Is it necessary to go through more of this hardship?* **Does anyone get a benefit out of my repetition?** No and *No one* really does. It is our instinct to leave an offspring, but no one seems to get particular benefits out of overpopulation. I detest crowded places, though I was not like this when I was young. After I became 40, I started hating crowdedness and loud noises more each year. During the COVID quarantine in 2021, I was happy to be in our library alone, as I was virtually the only one in the building. I literally experienced from hell to heaven in the same spot. I believe a country like Bangladesh is anguished: **Not because of poverty, but more of crowdedness.**

* * *

Currently, I am reading *12 Rules for Life* by Peterson. It's only *theoretically* well written in my opinion – no *practical* solutions. The author has been a Harvard professor for 30 years; his suggestions are not realistic, especially to the middle class in our society. The book starts with a story about lobsters, which have been on Earth for over 400 million years. He explained that even they have a sense of social hierarchy deep in their brains; every animal has the sense in common, including humans. So he suggested that it is important for us to "stand up straight with our shoulders back." Apparently, this straight posture shows others the sign of a winner and will prevent possible conflicts with them – a great scientific point, but wrong solution.

Earth has too many animals, but too few ideal shelters and resources for them. Which is why fighting happens everywhere all the time – in classrooms, Ukrainian borders or wherever. According to the book, after fighting, the winners stand up straight and the losers shrink their postures, which has happened throughout history on Earth. So is showing bossy a solution? I still believe that everyone gets hurt one way or another in fighting. The better solution is that **we should learn how to give up for more after having enough.** That is what intelligent *Homo sapiens* should do; otherwise, there is no difference between men and lobsters. I believe having a dominating posture may be effective to defend ourselves, at most; being competitive or working harder is not the answer; we will only get injured more if we keep exposing ourselves in conflicts. I think we should lessen greedy attempts, if there is no point getting more; we are not the robin as in the book. It is time to think differently, as modern humans who have evolved from the original *Sapiens* 300,000 years ago (not like *Australopithecus* had 4 million years ago).

People often put themselves in danger not because they need something, but because they want more: **Greed is the enemy.** While a few are excellent at keeping in good posture, others lose: these triumph and defeat cycles have caused misery for all of us; everyone loses this way in the end. **We should learn how to**

stop when enough; control makes things better for everyone – including every animal, plant or other life on Earth. Sadly, most books have been written to benefit only humans these days. Peterson was once on a talk show and the host asked, "How many children is ideal for a family?" He answered, "I don't think one is a good number." He said children can learn from each other when parents have *two* – nonsense as families do not live separately in a prison cell. He answered "two" since he has two. Or two is fine since Canada, where he lives, is totally empty. We cannot expect practical advice from an Ivy professor for fathers worrying about daycare tuition. I strongly believe one child in a family is the way to go. Earth will be super crowded in the end, which *can trigger extinction faster*. **Reaching overpopulation slowly is for both humans and other lives on Earth.**

* * *

The summary: "Having a lot of babies is the number one reason for poverty and social problems. Earth is already crowded and depleting enough that no family needs to have more than one child any more. 1.2 billion of the new population will be generated by 2040, so people don't have to try hard." Humans have caused miseries on other humans; people talk about Jewish holocaust or African slavery. However, did you notice that tons of animals are born to live only a couple of months and *butchered*? We can be vegetarians to help them. Or more ultimately, we can have fewer babies, too. The human population will be over 9 billion, regardless if I have one or two; one more baby can contribute to killing an extra 100 chickens – a meal for us, but a life or death for them. Simultaneously, I am glad I have one since I have been less stressed out financially. Conclusively, **having fewer babies is a win-win situation**: Good for my stress relief, chickens and the Earth's environment, including limited resources.

In a sense, no one *needs* to have a baby any more: **No animal on Earth has such an obligation, to begin with.** My daughter was born when I still owned the video game store, which was small (900 sf) in 2010. I barely made a monthly rent of $1,200 then, so I could not hire anyone throughout the eight years. My wife taught at a music school two days a week, located in a music store. She was so popular that her schedules were all booked completely from morning till evening (no lunch break) for those two days; I heard that, rarely, some artists didn't have a single student there. I had double duties on those days: taking care of my store and *baby daughter* together. We set up a baby room with the "pack and play" crib from Greco in the back. I had a hard time whenever a good amount of customers flooded in, all at once. That had happened all along for the last four years of my store life. We never knew what would happen in 10 minutes that place – empty or crowded. I was busy with eBay sales[5], too.

The store had a big screen TV for video games; I used to watch reality shows like "Jon and Kate plus 8" or "Nineteen plus counting." I was curious how others can take care of 6 identical babies or 19 kids in a family. Taking care of one had been more than a struggle for me (still hard, even though my wife takes care of her mostly). Eventually, humans have conquered the Earth and become the most dominant species. On a large scale, it is devastating that the top of the food chain is getting bigger. Most conflicts happen fundamentally because too many people share too little resources. On a personal scale, once we have a baby, we generally face two issues; firstly, we cannot work ourselves since we have to take care of the baby. Secondly, our spending becomes double for the extra member.

* * *

Like many of you, I had pressure to have two babies in my 30s. It came from everywhere: parents, wife, friends, etc. Physically, I

---

[5] A top rated seller since 2003.

was able to do so. But I am glad I have stuck to my own opinion and managed not to have more. In fact, having one child turned out to be the best decision I have made, after all. I closed out my video game store when the lease was over in 2014. I took a break for 1 year and found a job in a nursing home nearby in 2015. After working there for 7 years, I resigned in 2022. The place had been worse every year and eventually filed Chapter 11 bankruptcy in 2023 – its kitchens had so much food waste all the time. The weekend dishwasher job was fine only in the first 2 years. Then, a horrible Mexican sous chef came and things got unnecessarily stressful.

I tried to transfer to other departments after getting a medical coder license in 2018, which didn't work out for gender discrimination I suspect. The director of health information was a snobbish woman; all the workers and receptionists in that department were women – *every single one of them*. I did not make a big deal, since it was not a pleasant or high paying job, anyway; the woman director was fairly obnoxious during the job interview (I saw so many women quit that seemingly easy job afterwards). Moreover, I was overqualified with certificates, not required there – nonsense for me to try hard to share an awkward time with the boss.

COVID hit two years later and the dishwashers got even shorter in the nursing home after 2020. I tried to transfer to a wait staff only to avoid the horrid sous chef, but it did not work out again for any reason I could understand. I had worked two positions for the last 8 months there: the weekend dishwasher and weekday morning waiter; I was not able to transfer to the wait staff completely for any reason. I felt it seems the entire managers in that nursing home tried to force me to be a dishwasher, as it was severely short. Finally, a new company came and took over the entire dining department in 2022; I did not know there was a transfer deadline to the new company. I was scheduled to take a pharmacy technician exam around that time, which I passed at the first try. I told them I can still work as a dishwasher only on Sunday if they still need me. They said the transfer deadline had passed and suggested a slightly lower hourly rate; I wrote a resignation letter and quit. It was a bad job in many senses: toxic chemicals to my skin (cancer causing), low quality managers, etc. Truthfully, I have been wealthy enough not to get any job at all then; my investments have grown all along.

Still, do you know what I was glad the most when I got out of the nursing home completely? Getting enough dividends to cover my expenses? Having earned two certificates? My wife has been working all along? Above all, **I was glad that I have only one child to support.** During the 7 years, I had witnessed that good guys stuck in that dreadful job. Joe and Riccardo had four kids each – these two were nice guys, but had worked for two different jobs. I feel truly sorry for them since the working environment there was hostile, harmful and unfair – *hell created by humans*. We may see more career changes from now, as people live longer. When people lived only until 60, people never really changed their professions and passed away right after retirement. Soon, "the average Joe" may live up to 100. The number of kids we need to feed will matter whenever we change our jobs for any reason: job loss, economic depression, better positions, ambitions, etc.

* * *

I think hardships have two types: ***given and created***. If we are born in a poor family or have a sick mother to take care of, these are *given* hardships. But if you create four children and struggle to support them, those are hardships created by you. While we can have hardship, **we do not have to create one.** There was a woman cook named Roza in the kitchen of the nursing home – a Cuban Mexican single mother with a lot of tattoos and piercings; I never liked her since she was always *disrespectful* to dishwashers. She had 'a mom with liver cancer' and five children to support (from three different fathers). **Her sick mother is a given hardship; her five kids were a hardship created by herself**; I heard her complaining about money multiple times.

Still her action to create more kids could be beneficial for our society, right? Not necessarily. She got fired in 2018 and I believe the reason was drug addiction. She probably has taken welfare checks since her Facebook showed she had been at home all the time with two toddlers; it's not necessarily advantageous for the Treasury department. And her children can be troublemakers later on, as the mother was not sane – building more prisons can be another tax waste. In conclusion, I don't believe her actions to create five kids was inevitably favorable for society. Nonetheless, are her children happy, at least? I doubt it since they had been without fathers or enough money all along. Ultimately, producing five kids was not optimal for her own wellbeing, society or even children themselves. I don't think any baby wants to be born in that family – not fantastic in poverty. No one gets benefit, while Earth gets exponentially depleted.

Life is harsh already – true for all the animals on Earth. I used to think whatever happens in our lives is mostly luck, probably true only until we become 20. Now, at the age of 52, I can say **we are the ones who decide our own destinies.** *Having a hard time ourselves doesn't necessarily mean others get benefit out of it* – we can make our life grueling or we don't have to. At least, we have a choice.

* * *

Summary

1. We don't have to push ourselves to have a lot of children.
2. Regardless of whether I have one or two, the human population will be 9 billion soon. I could have had a harder time if I had two.
3. We don't have to sacrifice ourselves to deplete resources faster.

3

Getting into Debt Too Easily

If money is a religion, debt is a cult.
-Brad Kong

Getting a debt happens *when stupidity meets greed*; the smart but greedy don't have debt; the stupid but humble never have it, either. Only the stupid but greedy get it. Believe it or not, not paying a debt used to be a felony – common to go to prison for it in Europe. People still go to court, when they file a bankruptcy: Why? It used to be a crime. I use two credit cards everywhere, though I always pay up my balances; I cannot live without them, although the reason is convenience for me. Still, it's worth thinking one more time before signing up for a big one like a mortgage – basically, people pay more for the same things in the end.

There is a book, *"Debt: The First 5000 Years"* by Graeber. It explains that debt was invented during the Sumer civilization in Mesopotamia[6] about 3,500 B.C. The concept of debt is recent, since it was formed only 5,500 years ago. Humans started farming about 10,000 years ago, despite that we have been on Earth up to six million years. It has been normal for humans not to have any debt most of our history. I think the smartest thing I did *with money* was buying my condo *"in full"* in 2013. It is hard, especially when we live in the east or west regions in America; typically, the house prices there are twice higher than in the Midwest where I live. In 2008, the subprime mortgage crisis broke out and it lasted about five years. A huge amount of foreclosures and short sales came out on the market and these

---

[6] South central region of Iraq in 2023.

dropped housing prices significantly. By then, I had lived in rental apartments for about fourteen years. I had about $80,000 emergency fund my parents gave me after my daughter was born, all of which I saved in CDs. The price of a one-bedroom condo tanked to $60,000, so I bought one quickly.

One *advantage* to buying a home in full is a *discount.* The nice Polish couple owners[7] said they had two houses and were in need of cash. I got a $5,000 discount[8] immediately, when I suggested a cash payment. I used to pay $900 a month for apt rent by 2013 (a one bedroom rent is over $1,600 a month in Chicagoland, as of 2025). Now I pay about $430 HOA fee (association fee) a month, so I believe I am saving about $1,200 a month – the annual saving of $12,000 a year after deducting $2,000 property tax I pay, as a condo owner. I have lived here close to 13 years now, so over $150,000 has been saved only by not having a rent. I will save even more if I stay here longer.

It shows that the average lifespan of males is 78 years in America in 2024. It's long to spend 30 years on paying mortgages in that sense – spending most of our adult lives on paying for a house. I could have gone for a two-story house with a mortgage in 2012 (I am glad that I didn't). In general, housing costs much more with debts. Besides, I couldn't have been a writer if I had chosen that option; I could have worked for a medical coder full-time, which I do not care about, only to pay a loan. *I couldn't let myself waste three decades that way.*

* * *

Debts are everywhere these days: a mortgage, car loan or credit card – the major three types. Personally, I don't have any of those. I am using two cards all the time, but the balances are

---

[7] I am glad they removed the stove in this unit, a fire hazard making this 850 sf condo even smaller. Without them, I wouldn't have known we even have that option.

[8] The original price was $65,000 in 2013.

always $0 at the end of month. It is not like I am rich – I just don't spend a lot. Slavery from Africa might have been over 200 years ago; now geniuses have invented a new serf system. **In this brilliant set-up, slaves don't even know they are ones.** It doesn't even matter if you are a black, white or yellow; if you are poor, financially illiterate (or *both*), you get sucked in. Some wait in line for hours to get into the traps; some show off they got in. Frequently, I wonder if those "Korean *trolls*" don't know how to use a calculator (*'not graduated elementary?'*). **We pay more for the same;** some gnomes were even proud to have mortgages since they believe everyone has it – only 60% of Americans have them.

To me, there is nothing really worth trying with debt. Obviously, we need to use debt somehow during our lifetimes. But, *no debt,* **whenever possible.** Debt has had a lot of names: "balance, credit, margin, remainder," etc – merely fancy names of "leftover, business, investment and card debt," supposed to make us feel better or confused. Having debt used to be terrible even decades ago – a natural part of our lives these days. I have never paid any interest on my cards for a decade now; instead, I get cash backs from both every month; my spending limits are about $20,000 from both combined. I had a car loan 11 years ago, but was paid off within 3 months in 2014.

* * *

It is proven that people cannot focus on their jobs when they have worries: How do we get them constantly? One way is having a debt, distracting us regularly, so we make less in the end. How can we know if our lives are going in a positive direction? A couple of barometers to check that straight: our weights and debts. No one gets skinny automatically these days – weight loss requires controls and disciplines. We are less likely to spend a lot on medical bills that way. The other indicator is our debt situation in my opinion. Do you own a home outright without having a mortgage or rent? Then, definitely your life has been constructive so far – you might not be rich yet, but on the way. Paying for a house in full requires financial knowledge, savings and luck. **While smart people hide their wealth, stupids *pretend* to have it with debts** (e.g., luxury cars with auto loans) – idiotic from a perspective. I know a couple of Korean mothers whose children got kidnapped after pretending to be affluent[9]. Showing-off can offend others for no reason, while losing money on loan interests ourselves.

Unfortunately, I've never had an amicable relationship with my father. However, I admit that he was right about one thing: **No debt.** When little, he frequently said to me and my brother that, "Your dad does not have a debt." He has been unpleasant to deal with, but his voice changed tenderly whenever he mentioned it. What he meant by "debt" was "business debt," by the way. Using a debt to buy a house or car was out of the question to him (always using full cash). *He is the one who made $20 M from scratch.* Those old Koreans did not have anything, after the Korean war 70 years ago. While most Koreans are not as rich, "no debt" policy seemed to work out for him.

I found a Buddhist maxim online the other day: "Pain is not holding you; you are the one holding the pain. If you cannot save yourself, no one can. We are the result of the thought in the past – we will become the person in our thinking." The Dalai Lama also once said, "Humans are created to be loved and stuff are created to be used. Stuff are being loved and humans are being used nowadays." This applies to materialism, but especially true to cars and houses.

* * *

There was a Korean internet community I used to go to; trolls there were stupid and spending-wise. They all seemed to make traditional, but boring financial mistakes – very typical lives,

---

[9] The movie *Secret Sunshine* is based on true stories.

including full time jobs, mortgages, car loans, two cars, *two* children, wives with *no* job, etc. I'd never expected a maverick, but I was amazed at how they live so monotonously without any twist at all. Some tried to argue with me, despite that they all pay double on their house through mortgages. There is nothing wrong with it technically; using a mortgage is reasonable when even the cheapest houses are too expensive (i.e., San Francisco). In the community, some bought big houses with the hope that their prices would spark up soon. Currently, the single (unmarried) population is increasing fast and less likely they will buy a huge house. Virtually, house tags never go up more than inflation, but probably condo prices increase faster, as the single prefer and can afford small units.

Most of us get debts unconsciously. A majority of people turn frugal after being burned by a debt somehow. I used to be a waster myself, especially during the time I owned a business; during the *Cyb Knight*, I owed up to $9,000 credit card debt in 2009 – a business debt, not really from personal consumption, though. My mother saved me once and I have never had the same problem so far. I live frugally even without a car now.

The second biggest reason why people cannot quit a horrid job is a persistent debt – probably, mortgage is the most common. To me, buying a big house to show off could be a worse reason than having multiple kids, the #1 reason to force us to put up with a hellish job. **Debt will never bring us a profit.** Some trolls declared living in a bigger house means better quality of life – this is stupid. **Bigger houses only guarantee more chores** – we may or may not be happier, as houses quickly turn into a nightmare, too (some building problems are impossible to fix). In reality, debt can seriously lower our quality of life, as nothing is more important than peace of mind.

* * *

Summary

1. No debt as possible.
2. Not having a debt had been perfectly *normal* in history.
3. See if you can buy a small house in full – getting a complete homeownership has been a life changing benefit for me.

4

Not Using Systems Already Paid For

We should use what we already paid first.
-Brad Kong

There is a group of movies titled the *007 series* (*James Bond* films) – the first one was "*Dr. No*" released in 1962. Since then, 24 more have been directed by 2021. There are thousands of action movies released every year and unfortunately, most fail commercially. Still, if a movie comes with a prefix title of 007, it beats the competition. The similar examples are *Mission: Impossible* or *Harry Potter* series. An obvious example to use systems they already built is franchising.

The same goes for books. One of my favorite writers, Bryson, has written 19 books by 2023. Oddly, it doesn't seem any of his books have a relation to each other; one is about his childhood and another is about travel or the human body. In my opinion, he could have made more sales if he had arranged them in a type of franchise; for example, universe and body could be in *Bryson's science* series I and II. When readers see II in a book title, they assume there is I, which is an automatic advertisement without spending extra. Besides, some fans have preferences to collect all in a series. Some authors do this, even though many have published multiple books. In worse cases, some don't even use the same pen name. At least, Bryson used *the same name*, so people can find all of his works easily. We can apply this concept to our personal finances; in fact, we can be broke, when we don't.

* * *

I am a library *maniac* by nature; I have visited more than 30 libraries in Chicagoland so far. While the one in Schaumburg is probably the best, every library has its own ups and downs. One of my sanctuaries is the Wheelings – a hidden, but new building full of modern features. Mount Prospect has the latest bestsellers from Korea; sometimes, I wonder who manages the section (all carefully chosen); I feel the curator actually read those. Arlington Heights has decent interiors, near multiple restaurants in their downtown. Oak park has a huge comic section; the building has five stories and the entire second floor is dedicated to graphic novels. Koreans must visit the Glenview and Harold Washington in downtown Chicago – massive amounts of Korean books and I think only libraries in Korea have more than these.

(Image source: Starfield Library)

Only *some* of us go to libraries, while *all* have paid for them with property taxes. I used to work at a nursing home, only a quarter mile away from the library; my work hired about 1,000 employees. Strangely, I've never run into any of my coworkers there in the last decade (mostly cooks or servers). In this case, maybe I should say I was lucky, as meeting them could have been awkward. Still, you know what, though? *Maybe they still work there since they never go to the library*, which clearly helped me get two new certificates[10]. Do you know how I am certain all of us paid for the library *already*? Some think they are renting apartments, so have never paid property tax: **Apartment rents[11] already include any type of property tax**. Regardless, **there are people spending money "first,"** unconsciously. *It is more logical to use "free" first and spend if that is not enough.* Some check the library first, if there is a new movie coming out. Others check Redbox or Amazon first.

We have paid millions of things already, while <mark>some never use those and spend extra,</mark> unwittingly. Whenever I see my property tax bills, I find a good portion always goes to the community college nearby. There are students (including myself) going to a four-year university straight from high school, instead of finishing general courses in the CC, already paid by their parents who are homeowners or apt renters. Also, on the bills, nearly $3 billion goes to the water supply in our country each year – an extreme amount on ensuring the quality of water delivered to homes. However, some still order water from Hinckley or buy it at Jewel with additional charges: *Spending double is the reason for brokeness.* I used to buy millions of water bottles from Sam's club, while I owned my business. Now I carry a glass bottle to use drinking fountains at libraries, malls or hotels.

* * *

Another example is public transportation. Chicago homeowners reading property tax bills must find a chunk of the budget to go to public transits: subways, trains, buses, etc. Yet some Chicagonians only drive a car, as their sole ride. <mark>On top of the transportation charges, they spend extra on cars</mark>: loans, insurances, registrations, parking, gas, repairs, washings, maintenance, etc. D*ouble spendings*: one is on public transportations and the other is on cars.

---

[10] Medical coder and pharmacy technician.
[11] Apartment rent = property tax **+** rental profit

Some cannot live without a car for jobs, though (delivery guys, construction workers, etc). Whenever I check my property tax bill, I see only about $1 M goes to our library every six months – too small out of a total $6 B budget (6 months). Our library has played a crucial role as a town square for villagers, having done fabulous jobs. They deserve at least $5 M a year, still tiny, since over $12 B collected annually – nonsense that the park district gets over $100 M, while the library gets only $1 M.

The next example could be the trolleys in this village. We have a big shopping mall area and *free* trolleys connecting major spots: Woodfield mall, Street of Woodfield, Ikea, hotel, etc. I am the only passenger in the clean transit, nine out of ten times. We had the COVID pandemic for three years by 2022 and the federal government sent us stimulus checks, then; some never got those since they didn't file taxes properly – missing the $3,500 they could have gotten legally.

The last example is the swimming pool in my condo complex, right in front of my unit. I have paid for the pool through the HOA association fee every month in the past 12 years. Honestly, I have never used it myself, which has been a waste. But, after my family moved back in 2017, my daughter has stayed there up to 10 hours a day during summer. I think it is smarter to use it, instead of going to a village pool, paying a $10 fee. Actually, local friends can come here, too, but some go to Atlantis in the Bahamas, paying air tickets. **What they get could be more stress and waiting in lines –** lines for concierges, airports, rental cars, etc.

How can we be wealthy if we keep spending double? Chicagoland has myriad CTA[12] and Metra stations, and bus stops; not only free trolleys, there are free vans for seniors. It is walkable with all those transportations and uber, so my family has lived without a car since 2017. If we are short of money, despite working, we need to check if there is a spot we spend *double* on. There is a

---

[12] Subway.

reason, when your income melts away like snow in the summer blaze.

* * *

Summary

1. Do not spend *first* on everything.
2. Check if there is something you already paid for.
3. See if you can plan in advance to save.

5

Triple Spending Style

*If we are short of money, working "full-time,"
something must be wrong from the bottom.*
-Brad Kong

Anders Hansen is a psychiatry specialist from the Karolinska Institute in Sweden. He accepted 100 volunteers before 2016 and conducted an experiment – letting 50 people do one-hour walking exercise three times a week for 12 months; he let the other 50 do only stretching without walking. When he checked their brains, the result was striking: Hippocampus in the brains of walking people increased +2% on average while those of "stretching-only" people shrank -1%. He suggested that **walking helps our brains grow** (regardless of age) and **limits the dementias.**

What do you believe makes us walk less? Driving. Most Americans spend practically fortunes on cars (e.g, buying, fueling, repairing, cleaning, etc). Then, many spend *again* on dementia treatments later in their lives. **This is a *double spending*** in a sense: car and hospital costs. *Is it possible if we live without a car and walk for brain health*, from the start? Then, it's *double saving* – saving from "not owning a car" and "not staying in a memory care," when we get old. Some buy doughnuts, eat them and go to dentists. Or others do not buy a doughnut from the start and not go for implants. I noticed **some spend triple all the time for the same results.**

Those *who spend double* rather live on emotion than logic. Let's assume everyone goes to the library everyday; I live about 1 mile from one and always go there by walking – taking about 25 minutes, which is a good exercise itself. However, some go to the library by car, gym by car, spend money on gym membership and then do walking exercises there. **It is *quadruple* spending for the same result:** gas consumption; gym memberships and clothings; electricity on treadmills, etc. Similarly, a lot of people go to work by car and jog after work: Why don't they just ride bicycles to work from the start, so they can save on gas and time after work?

On the contrary, I witnessed some smart use their talents at work. When I was in downtown Chicago, I saw a construction site near the Willis tower – building a ground expansion of the skyscraper. For an hour, I had observed how the tips of new building frames connected manually[13]. What struck me was a muscular guy trying to connect two huge beams by hand; he seemed to be the type going to the gym everyday; apparently, his job also provided him plenty of things to lift the whole day. Another example is the Bloomingdale trail in Chicago, which is a walking bridge; I saw myriads of people go to work by bicycles and kick scooters.

* * *

I wonder how carnivores were created, originally; it must be painful for them to survive, as they have to kill others, whenever they need to eat; this is an offensive way to live on Earth. On the contrary, the lives of herbivores or omnivores seem to be less harsh, as plants they feed on don't move. In this sense, the creatures living in the least offensive way could be scavengers; they just eat whenever anything edible is found. I read that lobsters, living on the ocean floor, eat debris dropped from the surface – an example of living in the least offensive way. I believe this is how they have survived for more than 400 million years – by **not bothering others, and being helpful to clean environments.**

Modern humans are obscenely wasteful; we have the most offensive way of lifestyle on Earth. It is not like the poor are frugal,

---

[13] There is no other way.

while the rich are lavish – we all are *prodigal* to some points. We do not see animals like humans *in the wild*: Why? **Wasteful ones must have been extinct already.** Nature does not allow animals to be from thriftless – humans won't be an exception. Our agriculture started about 10,000 years ago and if humans become extinct within the next 100,000 years, that is not a long survival span for a species; dinosaurs had lived through over 165 million years on Earth, still alive as birds. As from a biology book, humans will be recorded as *"The shortest, but most impactfully lived species."*

People can live up to 100 years these days. A lot of people used to die before 40 even in the 19th century. Some know the painter, Van Gogh, died at 37; did you know his art dealer brother, who supported him financially, died at 33 as well? As people start living longer, I do *not* think we should live extravagantly any more: In fact, we should live as frugally as possible; otherwise, we may not be able to hang on to our money all the way up until 100. Simply, we are given more years to spend money. When we hear, "an old person died," we automatically assume that he or she passed away naturally. But it's possible that **a portion of seniors' deaths can be actually suicides, falsely reported as natural deaths.** Statistically, it shows houseless or *van dwellers*[14] die earlier; I suspect death could be a way for them to *graduate* from their painful lives; in the future, this could be true for the entire race on a large scale.

* * *

The weekend dishwasher job at the nursing home was physically hard, especially in the beginning – a mile from my home and it took about 30 minutes for me to get there by walking. After getting the medical coder license in 2018, I wondered if I should keep the job even for weekends; luckily, it was stressless in the first few years. I concluded, 'I can consider it as weekend gym exercises for eight hours; the only difference is *I get paid and receive free meals.*' It's true that I have lost a lot of weight and become more muscular after

---

[14] Check *Nomadland* by Bruder.

starting the job; I was obese[15] and diabetic before. I had commuted strictly by walking throughout the 7 years to intensify my exercise. **Some spend money to lose weight, while others get paid for the same.**

It was hard for me to wake up early in the morning, especially during winters. I thought that it would be hard as well, if I had to go to the gym for 8 hours during weekends. **We can skip the gym, but cannot be late for work, so the job had been a better coach in a sense.** During the 7 years, there had been extremely cold or snowy days – horrible winters in Chicago: 'Well, some go to Mount Everest after spending a fortune; let me consider that I am doing winter climbing in Colorado today.' The thirty minute adventures to work didn't look terrible relatively – the commutes were over quickly. Additionally, the job has assured me the reason why I should not waste money. I still feel sorry for those doing it for a living, though.

Particularly, I felt sorry for a Mexican boy named Omar in his late 20s; he had done it for a decade, then. I used to say to my wife that, *"The only crime he committed was being born as the first son in a poor family."* It is sad that **"born destitute" is such a crime to get that kind of punishment**, as the job was painful enough to be a penalty, especially over the winters. He was noble to accept his hardship without a complaint and helped other coworkers feel pleasant. I wish Latinos would breed less blindly, so less children would get penalized like that.

When I was in college, there was a Ukrainian girl who had worked at Disney World for a summer. She wanted to have a vacation there, but could not afford it – smart for her to work there, get paid and enjoy vacation together. I believe similar things happen in cruise lines as well. To write this book, I could have hired low incomers to listen to their stories. I read the graphic novel, "Jungle", originally by Sinclair, about Lithuanian immigrants working in Chicago butcheries during the Great Recession; their hardship got intensified after their child was born; in the end, Sinclair actually hired the protagonist in

---

[15] I used to be up to 165 pounds, but 125 pounds now.

the novel to listen to his story. Alternatively, I think **the author could have worked in a factory himself and collected info, while getting paid;** some do the same while making money and others don't. If we keep being short despite working, we should check if we spend double on anything, unwittingly.

* * *

Summary

1. Try to walk, instead of driving; walking is a gas saving tool, but also a great exercise itself.
2. Try not to spend double for the same results.
3. It would be great if we can choose a workplace where we can use our passion.

6

Living in an Expensive Area

Our evolution speed doesn't catch up with civilization. -Brad Kong

Statistically, the east and west regions in America are about twice more expensive than the Midwest in terms of housing; I personally don't see a logical advantage to living there – nonsense to pay more to get to wildfires (west) or hurricanes. It seems more sensible to move from the coasts to mid-America, actually happening nowadays; Texas, Idaho and South Dakota have gotten the biggest moving-in populations since 2020. I live in Illinois, also losing population every year; I believe it's due to high state income and property tax. However, Chicagoland is still growing, so I guess I will keep staying here for reasons.

First of all, the living cost in the Midwest is still *lower,* even after high taxes. Though not widely known, property taxes are <u>small</u> for condos in Illinois; I own a condo and it has been less than $2,000 a year after homeowner's exemption. Secondly, I bought my place during the subprime mortgage meltdown in 2013; I cannot find a residence cheaper in a decent neighborhood any more. It's hard to let it go, since I will never get it back for the same price ($60,000). Thirdly, the city of Chicago and its vicinity have the third biggest population in America and provided me plenty of places to walk (my greatest joy). Besides, the city has old, but well established public transportation systems, which helps me live without cars. I used to have symptoms of diabetes and walking has helped me stay away from it.

An expensive area may not be a good place to live *by nature*. Times Square may be the most expensive block in America and basically no one resides there. However, is it a nice place to stay? I will suffer from noise, crowds, pollution and bright lights all the time. We may have to spend more on rent to live there, yet it doesn't provide an optimal condition we can find in the suburbs. Although there is a difference on the discomfort level, *an expensive place* might be somewhat like Times Square; there is a reason when a place attracts people (i.e., scenic views); living in a crowded place comes with discomforts along with financial burden. Sometimes, I go to downtown Chicago to walk around. I would not visit my village necessarily, if I lived downtown. You know what, though? That is the reason why I feel happier to live in this suburb. *Since no traveler visits my village, I get more peace and less costs.*

* * *

Mental comfort is "much more" important than physical one. I believe everyone has his or her own sanctuary. When I think about it, it is about mental comfort. I like libraries in small villages – mainly because no one goes there – clean, but isolated, as not many even know there are such places. Not many are attracted, so I feel peaceful. The one in our village is too popular; people come from everywhere and many of the staff recognize who I am – mentally less comfortable, as I prefer being anonymous.

Most do not consider this mental comfort *seriously* when they buy a house. I happened to be in our neighbor's and found out that they do not have any trees covering their windows. I felt like I was standing on a podium in front of the audience. In my unit, three windows are covered by four trees; I always feel laid back and hidden. In my opinion, *it is not a coincidence that owners change every few years in the neighbor's unit.* On the contrary, the previous owner in my unit had lived for 23 years until she passed away. Since the longer we own a house the more profitable, it's important to check if we feel peaceful before buying a house. Some focus on how the home looks to others (fancy enough?). Some get an awful amount of debt to disguise themselves looking opulent. They actually put themselves in more vulnerable situations, including getting a thief or collection call from banks after all.

Personally, I've always thought NYC is the worst place to live in America. I graduated from SUNY at Buffalo and had visited NYC more than 30 times by 2006; the city has a big Korean community, too. My conclusion? Expensive, but unkind and dirty. I had visited dozens of other American cities and most were cleaner, cheaper or safer. A few were as expensive, but it was nice like San Francisco. I could have settled in NYC in 2006 (upon graduation), if the cost of living was cheaper at least. But *it was absurd to pay more to live filthy* – getting smaller spaces for higher rents. Whenever I visited there, I always felt citizens were under stress – *overcharging from everywhere from restaurants to bridge tolls.* More cloudy weather than sunny during multiple visits. I have lived in four cities in America in the last 26 years: Rochester, Ithaca and Buffalo, NY; Chicago, IL. I have never lived in NYC, but it's far more pricey than others – the farther, the cheaper.

Have you heard of the "California exodus?" Over 80,000 companies have moved out from CA since 2012, including Tesla, Oracle, etc. High cost of living and State income taxes – a lot of those have moved to Texas, particularly the Austin area. There was a funny Mexican dishwasher named Vincente at the nursing home I used to work at; he was about 60 and had 5 children, three of whom live in CA already. Against the trend, he moved to CA in 2019 and works in construction now. The COVID, wildfires and droughts broke out one by one after he moved in, so I wonder if his decision was wise. There is a Korean website I used to go to. I got shocked repeatedly, whenever I heard their complaints about the cost of living there. A large number of people on that site were from Silicon Valley, the most expensive in America in 2024. Their salaries and house prices were unbelievable; they probably got paid more, but ended up with nothing as they spent all on mortgages.

There is a travel YouTuber, "Korean Jay." He visited a girl's apartment in LA and I got shocked that her rent was $4,300 a month for two bedrooms (2022); she pays literally 10 times more than I do, because she doesn't own a condo, living in the west. **It's all about population** – the majority lives in the East and West and the middle is empty. High density drives housing prices higher along with other costs. *Do we make three times more, when we live in the East and West?* **Not necessarily.** The minimum wages are similar, if not more in the Midwest. Which is why people move to Texas crazily these days.

* * *

I was about to graduate from SUNY at Buffalo in March 2006. Most Koreans moved to NYC or its surrounding areas then. It is the biggest city in America after all – more importantly, big Korean communities are there as well. But, at the same time, my girlfriend (wife) had studied for her doctorate program in Champaign, IL. Simply, I had to choose either going to NYC or Chicago upon graduation. By 2006, I had made income out of eBay for about three years. eBay was a bigger venture than Amazon once and used video games were sold particularly well. EB games[16] and GameStop were growing popular, too. I thought that I could open a similar business to GameStop, if I can rent a small space. The only difference was that I could sell games on eBay together, because I have been a power seller since 2003.

After checking rents in Manhattan, I concluded, *"There is no way I can go to NYC."* Store rents were like $10,000 a month for 500 sf in 2006. I wondered what kind of business I needed to open to make that much money every month (jewelry?). I ended up renting a "900 sf" store for $1,200 a month in Chicago suburb months later. In a sense, my wife saved me, since *she was the only reason* why I even considered the Midwest. If I chose NYC, my life would have been much different (in a miserable way). I still remember I saw a GameStop in Manhattan when I was in NYC for the last time in Feb

---

[16] Later, it was purchased by Gamestop.

2006. Could they charge higher in Manhattan? **I don't think so.** All the brand new Xbox 360 or PS3 games were $60 in America, including online, until I closed my store in 2014. If anyone charges more, players can order it from Amazon, $60 at maximum. But did the GameStop in Manhattan pay more rent than *Cyb Knight?* <u>Of course</u>**:** I really have no idea how they could survive.

With AI, people can do the same jobs everywhere in America now. People have traded stocks online everywhere without working in Wall street. Since traders make or lose the same amount, regardless of locations, *those who live in cheaper locations make more in the end.* Another example could be the writer of *Pachinko* – she is a Korean living in Manhattan. She makes the same royalty whether she lives in a countryside or city. **For sure, she spends more in Manhattan.** Regardless of region, people spend more, when they live near shopping areas. I see some apartments built right on top of malls. They look fancy, but it's easier for people to find some attractive, but not needed items while walking around.

(Image source: One complex on Roosevelt ave in Chicagoland)

Also, when people live in the middle of nowhere, they tend to spend more on gas; it is cheaper to live near some infrastructures, including supermarkets and public transportations.

* * *

Summary

1. Expensive places are often worse places to reside.
2. Buy a house for your own comfort, not to show it to others.
3. See if you can live in a cheaper State for the same job.

7

Social Media Addiction

We may show too much to enemies.
-Brad Kong

The Sun magazine reported that the English rapper, Mota Jr., was found murdered at 28 after receiving diverse tortures in Sesimbra, Portugal in 2020. Police learned that he had frequently posted his *billionaire lifestyle* on his Facebook; they arrested three suspects, subsequently. I guess the rapper might have the "Like" addiction – getting joy out of feeling respected, high *Like*s on social media. Philadelphia news outlined that a 50-year-old electrician Tony Harris was found dead at his home in October 2015; he posted a selfie holding $60,000 cash bundles on FB, too; three burglars visited a week later and shot him on head. In the case of the rapper, he tried to promote his music, at least. In Harris' case, there is no point. **Both could have been alive, if social media didn't exist.**

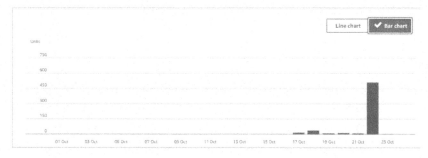

My first book *Introduction to UnBrokable** was released in October 2022 – a prequel sold 596 copies that month. I had finished the 5-day free book promotion on Amazon, allowing readers to download the kindle version for free. Still, it is *strange that 520 copies were sold only on one day. Why did most customers download only on the last day?* Statistically, about 4 million new titles are published in the U.S. annually (11,000 every day). About 50 copies were downloaded in the first four days. I was frustrated initially, so I opened the Reddit and Instagram accounts and started advertising there. I used a slightly different hashtag one day and *suddenly I saw 520 copies were downloaded.* Social media can be a powerful tool – not costing me anything upfront.

Some may ask, "What is the point of giving out free eBook?" The easiest way to sell 100,000 copies of a book is letting 1,000,000 people download it. Once they start reading the kindle version, some may want to buy the paperbacks, too. In particular, chapter titles in my kindle books are *not clickable.* I tried everything, but it never worked out. Readers may have hard times to go in the middle without the clickable contents links. After selling a lot, my free sales ranking on Amazon has jumped to 257th out of millions of books; as it goes up, more readers notice the book exponentially. When my book was just released, the ranking was like 2,000,000th. **How much money do I have to spend on ads to raise the ranking from 2,000,000th to 257th?** Most do not use social media this way; vainly, many use them to waste more time, lose jobs or even kill themselves.

* * *

Do you know what makes a woman attractive? She tends to be more attractive when she does not *show* everything; a lot of girls do exactly the opposite, unfortunately. Some may prefer an introverted girl. Regardless, *a girl tends to be more mysterious, when people have no idea about her.* Social media makes that *impossible*: **People show ugly things**, unwittingly. We won't recognize a garbage bag, if it has been there for a year. We all have such a thing in our lives and people see it through our postings. Also, your photos online won't make you look prettier in most cases – *only* get rid of fantasy. Any photo can show more flaws and these may be from your families, too – they are still linked and their embarrassments can be yours. **Social media reveals something we do not want to show one way or another.** It can still display vanities, often distasteful.

Here is one more thing, particularly a single woman doesn't know: A lot of men believe the *future face* of the girl is her *mother*, which is why some men check out their possible mother-in-law at least once. Strategically, it may not be a good idea for a girl to show her mother or grandma on FB: *No man is dying to get something turning out to be fat and ugly in the end.* Without seeing her mom, men imagine a fine old lady for the future (without this self illusion, there wouldn't have been a marriage and the human race would have gone *extinct*). By seeing her mom directly, a boy can hesitate approaching a girl even before dating. It is no coincidence that **the single, unmarried population increases fast along with the emergence of social media.**

Luckily, my wife and daughter don't have a social media account. Do you see my face anywhere except on my Amazon profile? **A girl's attraction goes to the maximum, when boys have no idea about her:** Brains of boys are wired that they make *positive* fantasies about a girl, when there is no info. One proof is the *Mask Fraud* phenomenon in Korea. People mandatorily wore masks during the COVID Pandemics for over three years and men automatically assumed that some girls are prettier when they cover half of their faces with masks. They joke that these girls are frauds since most look far less cute after removing masks ("Ma-gi-kun"). As social media gets popular, girls show more disappointing features than ever; for instance, I saw a girl's drunken father on FB once. She could have shown him later if FB didn't exist. But she reveals him in advance, before any relationship can possibly form. Boys stop approaching as soon as they see him (trashy father-in-law with tattoo?); then, she complains why she is still single at 40, as no one ever approached for life.

* * *

The nursing home I used to work at had two restaurants; I worked at the smaller one when I started the weekend dishwashing in 2015. There was a waitress named Vanessa in her early 20s; I ended up not liking her for her offensive boisterousness, breaking dishes. These are things I found on her FB:

- Her mother and she are alcoholics.
- Her mother is divorced with four kids.
- She is the second out of the four.
- She never went to college.
- Her mother does not have a job.
- Her mother met a Mexican man, working at a bodyshop, and they had the youngest son together.

I saw profanities by her all over; everyone was able to see what I saw. She was a Salvadorian descendant and eventually met a Mexican waiter, Alex, in the restaurant. *Both never go to community college* (basically free), but have two babies now. It seems both quitted their jobs from the nursing home at the same time, when she got pregnant. They both were in early 20s, but apparently did not have another job after quitting. Guess what? I saw all of those on her FB again. I never like these types of people – no job, no school, no income, but two babies – getting subsidies from the government for life. *Who does not know how to make a baby?*

After stopping working at the smaller restaurant, I began working at the bigger one from 2017. There was an Italian smoker girl, intentionally making loud noises in order to offend others.

One day, the trash spent 40 minutes in the kitchen making noises to annoy me; I filed a written complaint to her managers, who were absent that day. When I checked her Vine; some postings had disputes with her ex-boyfriend. These were what I found out through them, surprisingly:

- She had one abortion and two miscarriages.
- Her sister and she are both smokers and pot smokers.
- Her parents' house was *foreclosed* in 2010, so all were living in a rental apartment.
- Her sister was flying to Colorado to buy legal marijuana then, while their house was foreclosing.
- Her sister had a smoker boyfriend and broke up.
- She never went to college.

Apparently, there were five people in her family, including three adult children (all were over 30, including her). Couldn't they work altogether to save their family home from foreclosing in 2010? A small house with 3 bedrooms, so the mortgage could have been less than $2,000 a month. **There is no cure for those**; I would feel frustrated if my daughter spent money on air tickets to buy marijuana, while I was in trouble (her father passed away early in 2024). All these were giving out a scary amount of info to the public – a *disaster,* if it goes to the hands of enemies. What would they get as a result? **Nothing!** She also quitted the server job eventually and met an alcoholic husband with a tattoo and gave birth to a son; I found all these on Instagram again.

I know some people who used to go to *myspace* a lot (2005) and incidentally they were filthy poor. There was a girl in my biology class at SUNY and she started using it before 2005; then, the word *social media* was not even coined. She was from Elmira, NY and unpleasantly indigent; all of her hometown friends, including her obese sister, talking trashy, were penurious, too. It seemed she was the only one who made out to college. When I checked her Facebook long ago (2010), she still looked impoverished, after having two kids – diverse photos at friend's weddings in "bridesmaid outfits" – looking like clowns. She seemed to nail her coffin to be locked in destitution with her poor husband. For the first time, I sense *people cannot hide their poverty even in photos,* when they have been in it too long; her hubby looked out of work for quite a while (long dirty facial hairs). **Maybe brokeness became her destiny, since she had been with it for decades.**

Financially, only Zuckerberg makes money out of social media – did you know he hardly posts anything on FB, though? I have had only one FB account for decades, as far as social media goes (originally, opened for my video game store). I could not close that since too many childhood friends from Korea are connected to it (I have known them for 30 years). For sure, *FB has been helpful to find old buddies*; there used to be agencies finding people in Korea (sorts of detective agencies) and they used to charge a lot. Now they are all gone and it's a positive benefit from social media.

* * *

I think internet addiction can be detrimental, as we inevitably encounter trolls. We come across low lives more *online* than in real life for an obvious reason – *normal people do not kill time there as often as losers.* Some trolls are the true bottom garbage class – a loss to mingle with them or get assimilated. I have written on diverse sites in the past 30 years; not many, especially Koreans, appreciated my articles. It has been a waste, although it brought me a bit of fame only in the cyber world. Along the way, I met too many trash and suffered. On top of it, writing online never brought me any monetary gain, even though it might have helped my writing skills somehow. I finally bought 110 ISBN numbers ($870 in 2022) and started publishing books now.

Some experts suggested closing out all the social media accounts, unless we need them for a business. We can make others jealous, unintentionally. We offend the poor out of the blue, while we may not be that rich ourselves. Social media is the poor people's ground after all; statistically, less the rich or educated go there. We make more or lose less when we are in control. Some pioneers rushed into the internet industry and made a fortune. Most cannot do that, but, at least, we can reduce the amount of usage. Some poor browse the whole day, after getting an unlimited phone plan – I have a limited, but cheaper plan of "$125 a year" from Tracfone.

"N*ot losing"* is a way of "making" in a sense: **Not failing could be enough to be wealthy in real life.** We don't have to be stressed out to be productive. Often, not wasting is enough to be proficient. Have you felt exhausted for no reason? Social media is a black hole to devour our energy and time in a harmful way. There are sites helping me make money (e.g., eBay). Google doc, KDP and edit.org have assisted me with self-publishing. Authors used to go door to door of publishers, only to get their manuscripts published. As a writer, I cannot imagine bitter objections they had been through since there are plenty of obstacles even after publishing. On the contrary, social media put people in trouble – some lost jobs because of it.

Some check their phones a second more, as if they are full time slaves for the ads. **Checking social media consistently is like having "another job" without getting paid.** Personally, I never carry my phone outside my home – I have never lost my phone, thanks to that. It's unsafe to carry it all the time. While social media can be dangerous, especially when we have an enemy, **we don't even know if we have one or not;** we hurt someone, unwittingly; some are born hating everybody and I can be their target. In *The Art of War*, Sun Tzu wrote, *"If you know the enemy and know yourself, you need not fear the result of a hundred battles."* Writing on social media is exactly the opposite – revealing ourselves without knowing about an enemy.

* * *

Summary

1. See if you can leave your phone at home when you go out.
2. Let's give ourselves time to rest.
3. We need to use social media only for businesses.

8

Having a Bad Reputation

A bad reputation is a silent killer eroding our wealth.
-Brad Kong

A maxim in Korea: "A horse without legs runs for a thousand miles." I have witnessed some losers busy building more *disrepute* every day and staying poor. There were several dishwashers in the big kitchen and most were great guys. Still, I particularly didn't like two old Mexicans: Pancho and Enrique – ironically, these two were lifetime enemies with each other, but had few things in common. Both worked hard, but acted "boldly unfair" to others and rude – headaches for me throughout the seven years of my employment. Naturally, they had bad reputations, too. Both had been poor for life, although they were almost 60; they had been dishwashers for over three decades since no one helped them to move up. Both had been living in rental apartments "for life" and never had a chance to get a mortgage, not to mention buy a home in full. Thankfully, they were the ones giving me the inspiration to write this book: "**How to work to death, but stay poor.**" No offense, but they were Mexicans born in Mexico, while I had generally better experiences with those born in America.

People tend to get jealous easily, when there is no hope to improve their situations. Some live in a dead end forever; they often compare what they have with what others have now, since there is no room to get more. Losers waste time on being jealous, while *winners look for more profits.* One weird thing about money is that paying more brings worse choices sometimes. There is a reason when an item has been popular –

once it's everywhere, its price goes down. For example, choosing water for a drink is free in most restaurants – coincidently, the best for our health, too. If we choose a wine, it costs way more (often, more than a meal). Nonetheless, is wine beneficial? No – alcohol is notoriously bad on teeth. Chanel once said, "The best things in our lives are free." I do not agree completely, but **the least expensive things are occasionally the best** – *actually beneficial*.

When someone mentions assets, people automatically think of only *cash generating assets*: stocks giving out dividends, etc. But when we define an asset as "something putting money into our pocket[17]," there are other types as well: **experiences, intelligence and reputations.** These three could bring more than just profits, if we grow them wisely. *It won't necessarily cost us money to accumulate these.* I was passing by our village hall the other day and surprised at thousands of people watching a concert. The singer was Semple, known for *7th Heaven*. He was singing *It's My Life*, a Bon Jovi song, which didn't impress me. When I checked his name, he was an *American Idol* contestant in 2010 (only 70,000 clicks on YouTube). Yet it's an example showing the power of *reputation*. Only because he got famous once 13 years ago, he still attracts crowds and makes money overnight: *Being known to others (famous) is an asset.* We can be broke when we have a bad reputation.

Being kind does not necessarily cost money: "Kindness can be the most powerful, when we give it without expectation." Being kind is a way to raise our reputation without extra spending, although it's not always about money. We don't need to be kind to make money, but it's like **social insurance purchased by our actions**, as we need help from others to survive in the end. What does make a person *disreputable*? *When we act too selfishly*, we get it. Ultimately, **the extreme form of selfishness is betrayal.** There were three women who gave me bad impressions in the past decade.

---

[17] Definition by Robert Kiyosaki

* * *

There was a singer named P in Korea; she started career when she was a teen and had performed for over 20 years. I liked her 7th album released in 2007 and found her blog built for fans in 2011. Even though she was a star during her teenage years, she was a "no big deal," as she was over 30 by then. She was humble and replied to all the comments on the site in 2011; she replied to mine as well, which was stirring. One day, she finally got a minor role in a soap opera on TV in 2012. *Suddenly, she deleted the blog completely and acted as if nothing happened*; personally, I took it deceitful – she used the site to check if she is still sellable in entertainment. Gladly, she never got her fame back and completely retired, after all.

When I dug more, I felt like this has been her way of life. There was a time she had been a singer without any popularity for about 5 years from 2010. There was a CEO from an entertainment corp generously helping her get minor gigs. She was following him on her Instagram, only while she had a contract. *In 2020, she disconnected all these helpers and was following no one* (0 following). Since she still had 60,000 followers as a "celebrity," she could have benefitted CEOs by just following them, which doesn't cost money.

She got married in an egocentric way in the end. Due to her selfishness, she has been losing opportunities to make a fortune now: Why? Strangely, she married an old bold guy, already having two kids in 2020. There was a rumor that she had extramarital affairs with him before his divorce. As a result, she has not been on TV any more. Now she has one baby with the guy, but cannot be on one of those "raising kids TV shows", oddly popular in Korea. **I know it's not all about money.** However, if she got married to a normal single guy (not having an ex-wife or kid), she could have made $300,000 a year easily now for being on TV; Korean entertainment is huge, as it expands to other countries (as in BTS case). Now she has no income, due to her cumulative selfish acts and bad reputation.

She probably ends up divorced one way or another: One day, the husband will realize that money is the sole reason she chose him; there aren't others, when *a single woman* necessarily married a hairless man having two kids from his previous marriage. Even if there is, morally she shouldn't have done that (taking another woman's man). *She did not marry to support him or his two kids with her money.* The man will realize he is the sole one supporting all their big spendings: **Unfair relationships never last long**.

* * *

When I was in college in Korea in 1998, I studied CS as a minor. Since it was a minor instead of a major, I did not have many friends in those classes. There was a girl who approached me and asked many questions, who I found was accepted with the highest score to the department. However, there was an odd thing about her: *She always backed off immediately, whenever anyone asked her for help*. My friend also said this was the reason why he had kept his distance from her. I haven't seen her since 1999, but recall that she was quite selfish.

Lastly, Ariana in the nursing home: While I had worked as a weekend dishwasher for 7 years, I also worked as a morning waiter for 8 months in 2021. The restaurant was slow and I worked for only four hours from 6:00 - 10:00 AM during weekdays (two jobs). There was a young Latina server named Ariana, apparently friendly in the beginning. I had good feelings initially, but ended up staying away. Oddly, she approached the old Mexican (Pancho) in the kitchen aggressively. I kept my distance from her since I didn't want to get close to anyone on his side. Greedy Pancho had approached too many women all the time, so I didn't know what she was thinking.

When I resigned from the nursing home job in 2022, I gave my contacts to several coworkers. "A" was attending a nursing school with a scholarship, so I gave her my phone number to use as a reference, if she applies for another job – *a way to help others without spending money.* She texted me a week after I quit that she was applying for a CNA in a big hospital; then, she asked me to fill out 40 questions in a reference form for her, which I did gladly. I kindly added, "It does not cost me anything, so no worry." But, strangely, her text got silent right after my help. I did it quickly and even sent a confirmation to her. I asked for her email just in case, so I can use her in my reference likewise, if I apply for another job (I wasn't sure if I would be a writer, then). I asked twice, but she disappeared magically.

What is this? Letting me know her email won't cost her anything. Her email address is on Google all the time, but I just did not like her intention to take advantage and disappear in such an unpleasant manner. Her butt was extraordinarily big and didn't feel good about her (m*y intuition was right).* Being selfish blocks any good opportunity from coming in. On the contrary, being kind can save us and improve our situations, connecting with more luck. **We should be helpful, especially when it does not cost anything.**

* * *

My father has always been unpleasant to me for the last five decades – ready to be angry at any time throughout his life; I have always thought that it is a curse if someone is born with that much anger. While having been unpleasant, he has always insisted on me to take over his *fur business* in Korea; *it was stressful that I am even glad that no one wears fur coats any more.* Regardless, he could have saved tons of money from my education abroad, if we had a fine relationship. I went to colleges in America, partly to stay away from him.

Everyone hated Pancho in the nursing home, who reminded me of my father. He was a hard worker, and told me once that he was paying $1,500 a month for his two bedroom townhouse to rent. He has been renting for 35 years and never even had a chance to step in the bank to fill out a mortgage application. He has lost countless opportunities. We can give our kindness to people when we cannot give out money. My wife even gave a bunch of plastic bags to a kid who needs them on a regular basis; she is a born giver by nature. Just help people as much as you can, especially when it does not cost anything – most are not a betrayer and our favors come back inevitably.

* * *

Summary

1. Let's help others, especially when it does not require any money.
2. Keeping a good reputation is not all about money, although we get benefits from it in the end.
3. Being disreputable blocks all the possible opportunities.

9

Making Yourself Undesirable

A tiny flaw can blow out the entire plan.
-Brad Kong

There are two retired legendary pitchers debuting together in Korea in 1992: Chan-ho Park and Lim. Park had been the main pitcher in several MLB teams, including Yankees and Dodgers. Lim had reigned the Korean pro leagues over a decade and some argue that he had a better pitching skill than Park. However, I learned there is a massive asset difference between these two – the net worth of Park is about $40 M, while that of Lim is less than $10 M (2022): What has made the $30 M gap? Maybe the American leagues paid more than the Korean. Another obvious reason is that Park had been in a lot of commercials, while Lim had been in virtually none – Park is slim and handsomer. Lim has gained *massive* weight that I couldn't even recognize him[18].

I am not saying that we should look pretty to make more money. Nonetheless, there are people ignoring or even abandoning their own hygiene or appearance. Sadly, some turn themselves look *undesirable* for a job. More surprisingly, some spend extra to do that: **Some even spend money to look dangerous or ugly** (e.g. tattoo). Trying to look pretty is trying to survive in a sense: Do you know how to find out if our lives are in good shape? We can simply check our weights. Sometimes, I come across photos of old acquaintants on FB and get shocked by how much they gained: **Fitnesses tell a lot, since no one can change weight quickly.** If a fat friend has gotten skinnier, the person must have

---

[18] We went to the same high school.

improved: Why? No one gets thinner automatically – requiring control, mindfulness, knowledge or enough money. Losing weight is a way to make ourselves desirable in the job market, **which won't cost a cent, technically** – just fasting or eating less should be enough, as I have lost 40 pounds myself since 2014.

Our attraction could be our biggest asset; we make less, when we look, act or talk dirty. Also, keeping a decency matters, as people, especially women, have an instinct catching it as positivity. Our appearance will always matter (as we have eyes) – even to jobs not seemingly requiring good looks (e.g., dishwasher). Our physique will always matter until the last day humans exist. While plastic surgeries are *overkill*, it is important to keep ourselves as *neat* as possible.

As a man, I perceive skinny girls charming at first sight – an instinctual recognition I cannot control. I have thought about the reason why; maybe they are healthier or less smelly; maybe they fart or burp less; maybe they look more hygienic than oily. In the end, instead of making ourselves look better, **it is more *crucial* not to look bad**. Believe it or not, some spend money to look "*distasteful*"; some spend to gain weight or waste money to look less suitable for a profession and all these can lead to brokeness.

* * *

Maybe it takes a lot of money to be rich. Nevertheless, it doesn't take a lot to stay above poverty; at least, it hasn't cost me huge. Maybe I have been lucky, frugal, or unwasteful. I went to an Indian supermarket, Patel Bros, the other day. Some Mexican guys were collecting shopping carts in the parking lot. I felt sorry since it is one of the killing jobs – a hidden hellish one. Still I would say it didn't cost ample to get myself out of the dishwasher job; maybe it didn't bring me much to begin with. Or it's less expensive to live in the Midwest or I bought my house early, so I don't have high fixed spendings.

Regardless, *do not aim to be "rich"*; we can give up more easily that way. Instead, focus on staying away from poverty, more practical. A goal should be achievable, so life can be easier and more content, after all. I set up my goal to sell at least "1 book a day" for my publishing. Although I have sold 102 books a day before, I still set my target low – **just selling 1 book a day.** Staying away from lavishness has been more than enough for me to be fine, financially. Still, whenever I saw Korean trolls complaining about money, I could detect two distinct features from them.

1. Wasting time pointlessly (especially on being jealous)
2. Virtually all of them have a rent or mortgage, the most expensive waste (not a single soul among them bought a house in full)

These 1 and 2 seem different, but go mostly together.

* * *

There was a shooting incident in Highland Park, IL on July 4th, 2022. During the Independence Day parade, a low life named Crimo III (21) shot paraders from the roof of a building; six were killed and thirty-six injured. The shooter was on the loose only for hours, but got caught quickly; he had large tattoos on his face and neck, looking nasty; it's impossible to miss this guy if anyone sees him. There are people who don't need a job since they have more than enough for life. Still, we never know since people start living up to 100 years these days; it's possible that we may need one during life. Oddly, some even get a part time job to kill boredom in Korea and China (trivial stressless positions). Regardless, **not killing off our capabilities to make money is important**; at least, being able to get a job without restrictions wouldn't hurt.

One reason why some may not be chosen for hiring could be a tattoo or piercing. The big nursing home I worked at never really hired people with those. If it did, these employees must be placed in a position where residents cannot see them (libraries or village halls don't hire these, either). We may or may not be hired in any job: However, **why do we have to limit ourselves, to begin with?** Getting a tattoo or piercing is <u>*not free*</u>, anyway. Tattoo parlors are generally located in low income grey areas. Some make themselves even poorer by becoming *"unchosenable."* **When we are broke, isn't it common sense to save all the money as much as we can?** I had no room to waste on anything. *Why do they still spend money on tattoos or others and cannot get hired as a result?* Maybe they don't have survival instincts?

 When I worked as the weekend dishwasher, there was an annoying dining hall manager. She was unnecessarily demanding – never missing a chance to ask a favor if any blue collar worker was around. She seemed to receive a salary for nothing, while assigning all her job to others. Nonetheless, what surprised me the most was that she had a big black tattoo on her chest: 'How come such a person was chosen for the manager? Not appealing for white[19] retirees,' I thought. I assume she didn't wear showy clothes during her job interview.

 But you know what, though? She was gone for good, only after a year, rare in the place; I was happy (as if I got a promotion). Apparently, the company didn't extend her one-year contract. I remember she stopped by the kitchen one last time after she couldn't find a job anywhere else. She was annoying even for that 10 minutes, but she said she came to re-applying for the job. I overheard her conversation with E (a nice black cook); it was rude for her to show off that she would go to a mall, since everyone there was working double for Thanksgiving that day.

 Regardless, it seems she did not catch the real reason why she was discontinued: White seniors and a black girl with a breast tattoo don't match; she lowered the image of the organization. A little thing blew out her career, as she was a single mom desperately in need of cash. I personally have never felt an attraction to long nails some female rappers have; skilled professionals do not have those;

---

[19] She was black, while all the residents were white.

physical workers like cooks or flight attendants cannot have those, either. Who has them? Ladies not having a real job – Instagram models, background dancers, etc. Mothers having a baby would not have those, so super long nails are not related to much productivity, as well. Men, especially singles, should stay away, as they can hurt others physically, as the nails can turn into weapons, when mood swings in a bad direction.

* * *

Do you have a job you like to get hired by? While I owned the video game store, applicants came to ask for a job every single day throughout the 8 years until the last day (I never put a "help wanted" sign, though). People knew I was working alone. Or some might have thought the job was easy (true). Probably, over 3,000 came to ask and some even insisted on filling out application forms (we never had); I just gave them blank A4 for writing their names. I was not able to hire anyone since business was slow.

I still remember a morbidly obese guy asking for a job *repeatedly* (nothing wrong). Anthony was actually a nice customer in the beginning and brought a lot of his nephews to the store. I ended up not liking him since he tried to cut down item prices too aggressively. He was like 500 pounds and I thought he may not fit into the space behind the counter; all his teeth were noticeably rotten due to intensive soda drinking. I was relieved when he finally got a job for newspaper delivery; he said he was happy since the job has no aggravation. I remember his girlfriend and he worked for the Salvation Army during the Christmas season. They collected money in the red bucket and came to the store to buy a couple of games.

Plenty of jobs started available after COVID pandemic in 2022; a lot of people have passed away or been hospitalized; these days, we can self-publish books or videos on YouTube, too; which makes job applicants even less. Personally, I do not have any plan to be employed for the rest of my life: *Nonetheless, I prefer to keep myself employable just in case.* My driver's license shows that I was 165 lbs in 2007. I have lost about 40 LBs after kidney stones and a molar infection, subsequently. Now I am 125 lbs[20] and keeping in shape is just about respecting myself (*not losing hope*). I was surprised that my bank balance never went down during my fast (2009), which made me realize that I had spent an incredible amount of money on food my whole life. It is conspicuous that foods we eat do more harm than good these days.

* * *

Summary

1. It's better for us to check "if we are employable or not," even when we don't need a job.
2. Some spend to be *undesirable* in job markets.
3. Doing things mindlessly can lead us to poverty.

---

[20] 5' 6" feet height.

10

Marrying a Spouse Without an Income

Marriage never guarantees happiness.
-Brad Kong

(Image source: Field museum)

In 12 rules for life, Peterson pointed out an interesting fact: While human skulls have changed drastically in the last six million years, chimpanzee skulls have remained about the same. Humans and chimpanzees share a common ancestor named CHLCA[21]; the skulls of CHLCA and humans are exceedingly different, whereas those with Chimpanzees are similar. Anthropologists believe it happened because human females have been more selective than chimpanzees; biologists believe only half of human males have been able to leave an

---

[21] Chimpanzee–human last common ancestor

offspring somehow (ladies always try to find a stronger or richer partner even nowadays). The offspring are expected to be "better" that way, which is why the skulls of those two are hugely different, as a result.

However, are all those ladies good enough for men who they try to find? Unfortunately, **many are disqualified for marriage**, even though men are willing to accept whoever. Consequently, divorce rates are high everywhere, costly, especially to men. Nonetheless, it is true that I have been able to accumulate savings faster thanks to my wife. Whether we get along well or not, her income has been helpful. According to my experience, whoever we get married to, we face the worst moment eventually. Maybe there is nothing wrong; maybe this is just how human relationships go – *conflicts are inevitable when two people live in a space.* On top of it, couples' struggles are intensified after their child is born.

Two solutions to stay in marriages amid disputes: First, it's important for us to marry a partner who provides *solid reasons* why we should not divorce. Maybe she makes a lot of money or looks outrageously beautiful; maybe she has a doctorate degree or is a superb cook. The more reasons, the better it is, as when we avoid divorce, we get wealthier. Some men marry fattish girls from low income families having no job or degree – easier for them to get divorced, due to less reasons to stay in marriage; as a result, they get poorer than ever after the legal separations. Secondly, go easy on having more kids. Parents get more stressed out and squabbles, as they breed more.

* * *

Love is the most precious in the world, so should we kill for it? Or is it a hormonal interaction in brains to reproduce? Why was it created biologically billions of years ago? *Possibly, it was an initial impulse for animals to generate offspring.* Some writers exaggerate it to the maximum to sell romances. Wedding and jewelry industries are big, so they need to intoxicate someone to buy anything for sentiment. Fine, but there should be some limits, before ending up in miseries with scars (don't get me wrong since I am not a cold hearted robot). High levels of dopamine and norepinephrine are released in our brains during attraction (the same hormones when taking heroin). In the case of heroin, it strongly activates dopamine neurons; the same goes for nicotine (hard to quit smoking). So, from a chemical perspective, being in love is similar to being addicted to the dope; we may have to give up any harmful relationship before it goes vicious.

Realistically, men should not go too low for women: *There are women not showing any bright future*; we only sink together getting involved. Some women are smokers and drinkers; some don't have a job, or have one incomparably worse than their partners. Actor Cage has been married five times by 2023 and none of his wives have been a known actress; in fact, most had trivial jobs like waitress, makeup artist or movie extra (getting married to him was probably their biggest achievement). Instead of surrendering to the brief attachments, he should have been friends with them, since divorces must have been painful and expensive.

Also, it may be a better strategy for us to get married with a woman genuinely into us, instead of someone we like. The life after marriage may be more enjoyable that case – farther from hell, at least. **Never stick to a woman not interested in you.** *Don't think changing her mind is an accomplishment*; it is possible that she has never been a "prize" from the start; it is probable that she has been a nobody while you are just not her type. We lose a chunk of money or do endless chores after a wedding, if we make a wrong decision. Strange thing is that a girl is not necessarily in the high league, only because she is not into you; also a "high born" can be interested in you (rich girls can be in love with you or poor girls may be not interested in you). Statistically, husbands get wealthier faster, when their partners have a job.

I am not sure if it's a good idea to marry a too diligent woman, though; I am married to one who wants me to participate in house work, but it's hard for me to keep up with. Whenever I take some break, she preaches, "It's not fair and marriage cannot survive this way." and all that crap. Alternatively, I am trying to *reduce the total amount of work in the house*: having fewer babies, eating one meal a day, not owning a car, living in a condo without a yard, etc. Still, if a wife is industrious enough to make money (while taking care of home and child), that's great for the husband (super women exist). I don't create extra work for her, at least; **I've used my brain to reduce the total pie before slicing it.**

* * *

It is extremely hard to find a woman who a man can *trust*; I am lucky enough that my wife is a reasonable spender and money maker. However, more crucially, she is one of the few I can count on. Some go broke since they live alone – especially true for women, as many go for easier but lower paying jobs. As Peterson suggested, men dominantly go for harder, more dangerous, but higher paying ones. A lot of women, thankfully but unfairly, take care of their children or elderly free for years if not decades. This type of sacrifice usually doesn't happen to men, though I had served in the Army virtually free for 26 months.

Traditionally, older girls have a role to sacrifice themselves for their families, unfair. Apparently, it has been like this for millions of years. Some stupid men keep having babies and use their eldest daughters as babysitters. *It's like these girls have a full time job before going to school, while the entire family gets poorer.* This reminded me of Pancho – the fat Mexican dishwasher. His eldest daughter was working in the hellish kitchen, while becoming a free nanny for his grandkid; he has been idiotic, greedy for more women and stingy to male coworkers. Smart men already prefer not to have more, especially in the era of overpopulation. **Some just cannot keep up with civilization** – *it is the man's fault if his family is poor and faces a hard time this way.*

Some get poor since they marry the wrong spouses – no income, spending a lot, wanting more kids or *all combined.* Rather than getting the wrong, I would live alone. Finding a wife, making money, being frugal and wanting no child at the same time had been impossible for me – **less than 10% are in this category.** Some are kind, but do not make money, which I cannot blame. If they make some, they are not frugal, try to have a large family or something like that.

In Korea, a good portion of women quit their jobs right after weddings; **I feel they get a job only to lure a man into getting married** – pretending to be a career woman, but don't do anything after marriage; I do not understand why full-time housewives are so common, despite that Koreans are diligent. Equally, strange are Mexican women in my opinion; a Latino man (floor cleaner) said many produce a lot of kids no matter what. Life becomes hellish that way, whether we are rich or poor; we guarantee to live an overloading life since children bring all sorts of trouble. The cleaner mentioned some leave a man if he refuses to have more kids (crazy). For White or Black women, some have extraverted negative factors, spoiling marriages. In the nursing home, some screamed a lot which I have never heard from my wife; I cannot live like that, as I cannot be startled continually.

In a financial sense, there are countless wedding or bridal shops in America: Who are the customers? **Some women bring debt even before the wedding;** some have secrets, and men usually find those, when it's too late, causing the high divorce rates, subsequently. *Being single is better unless we meet a good partner.* Not being a male gold digger, but there is no reason to get married to a woman without a job, when 80% of them graduate college in this country.

* * *

Foreigners may find this weird, but some Korean men (especially old ones) not only don't allow their wives to work, but *encourage them to stay at home without a job.* Why do they want their wives incomeless? I am a middle aged myself now, but have never understood it. Presumably, they try to dominate power in the family. Those Korean grandpas, preferring jobless wives, are not necessarily wealthy. In fact, **many of them are poor just like Talibans insisting on tradition** – got stuck in prehistoric ideas. *Commonly, they do the same thing to their children as well.* When I was a teenager, my father always made sure that I didn't get a part time job during summers: *Did he give me anything to compensate for that?* **Not really.** I had been broke, while being forced not to work. If my daughter gets a part time job during summer, I might worry a little; it cannot always be pleasant to be at work. But she should learn it her way and I need to wait until she does not want it any more. **It is still stupid for everyone to be poor together in a family, while no one else is working except father.**

There is a Korean site I used to write on. There was a garbage troll wasting time on posting nasty comments. I had never seen him writing his own, but this is what I found out: He works for an IT company (unverified); he has a "huge" mortgage debt and auto loans; his wife and he never went to American college (no money for education, but debts for others?); having two kids; an alcoholic; no side income; no investment profit; calling cleaning ladies once a week; *his wife has no job*. Wait: *His wife does not have a job?* **Of course not.** No sane woman gets married to such a loser. Yet he paid for cleaning ladies for his wife, so now I can say that he is officially classified into the "Pong-pong men" category.

Pong-pong men is a slang coined lately in Korea. "Pong-pong" is a dish soap brand; now it implies men who do dishwashing, meaning taking care of "leftover women." It infers a man who gets married to a gold digger, who enjoyed her life fully with other men. In Korea, there are groups of parasites trying to find profitable husbands – often promiscuous and having no particular profession or education; they are considered as leftovers and some men are cleaning them out in the final stage because they were "fascinated" by their beauties. I can translate it to "duped husband" in English. It has been a big issue lately with a tough economy during the Pandemics. Korean men started realizing that giving all their salary to wives and getting a small allowance from them is ridiculous – shocking, but many actually live like that (they give all of his $3,000 monthly wage to their wives and get only $500 allowance from them). *Their wives have total control and anything is possible when we live* <u>brainlessly</u>.

In America, unwittingly, some make their wives unworkable by having too many kids (particularly the Latinos). How many babies are needed to make a mom *immobile*? Surprisingly, *two*, according to my experience. Daycare costs of <u>two</u> often exceed a typical woman's salary, so it forces her to stay at home. When I worked at the video game shop, I had seen a man talking over the phone to his wife to get permission to buy a game (they mostly had two). They had a *financially suffocating* life – I didn't want to count nickels and dimes, which is why I have one.

My wife has a nice coworker and she gave my daughter a couple of old American Girl dolls. They went downtown the other day and bought a "clothes set" for the dolls, which was $38, including clothes, shoes, a cupcake, etc (2022). If I have two, it could have been $76; I do not think I want to spend that for a couple of clothes sets. I am personally happy with one. I could have felt empty, if I did not have my own family. However, **I didn't want to pressure myself to make more, either.** No one will give me a medal of honor, only because I have two, instead of one (*no one cares)*. Earth has over 8 billion population already growing fast. More money won't cure every problem.

* * *

Summary

1. Never push yourself to get married.
2. Always stay awake – don't do things only because others do.
3. Try to marry a spouse with an income, as there are more jobs available at home with flexible schedules these days.

Author's Note

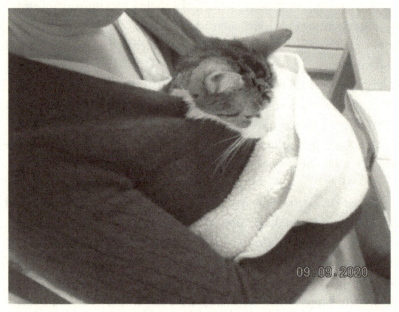

My wife is holding Oscar (2020).

Congratulations: I truly appreciate you finishing my book until the end. ***I would appreciate an "Amazon review!"*** *I do read all the reviews myself and try to learn from them. I wish my best luck to you!*